Cotton Theory™ Quilting

Quilt First – Then Assemble™

Book One
Cotton Theory Series

Betty Cotton

Cotton Theory, LLC
Osseo, Wisconsin

Cotton Theory Quilting

Third printing 2009
Second printing 2007
First printing 2006
14 13 12 11 10 09   3 4 5 6 7 8 9

Cotton Theory U.S. Patent No. 6,696,129

This book was produced and published by Cotton Theory, LLC

P.O. Box 22   Phone: (715) 597-2883 or (800) 673-8075
13900 7th Street   E-mail: quiltyard@quiltyard.com
Osseo, WI 54758   Internet: www.quiltyard.com

We welcome your suggestions and comments.

Publisher: Betty Cotton/Cotton Theory, LLC
Project assistants: Cindy Moores, Betty Nyseth, Katie Wolff, Sarah Wolff
Editor: Monica Stauber Holtz
Book designers: Andrew Clausen, Monica Stauber Holtz,
with assistance from Heidi Strosahl
Technical illustrators: Heidi Strosahl, Betty Cotton
Cover photographer: Shane Opatz
Room and project photographers: R.G., Shane Opatz

Embroidery designs by Cactus Punch, Pfaff and Oklahoma Embroidery Supply & Design
are used in this book with permission.

ISBN-13: 978-0-9772611-0-9
ISBN-10: 0-9772611-0-7

Library of Congress Control Number: 2005933510

This book is printed on acid-free paper.
Printed in USA

Dedication

To Cindy Moores,
who makes everything possible.
I am grateful every day for her support, encouragement,
and time in keeping pace with all I do.

Acknowledgments

Two years ago this book was just a dream.
With the help of wonderful friends, family, and staff, it is now a reality.

Many people contributed to the creation of this book.
I am truly grateful for their help and support.

Special thanks and appreciation go to the following individuals:

My husband and business partner, Jack Cotton,
for his patience throughout the years while I spent many, many hours
experimenting in my sewing studio.

My daughters, Sarah and Katie,
for their computer knowledge and appreciation of sewing and quilting.

My staff, Val, Norma, Teresa, Diane, Cathi, Terri, Cindy, and Vern,
for their devotion and dedication to educating all of the inquisitive customers
who pass through the doors of the Quilt Yard.

My students,
whose positive feedback, enthusiasm and enjoyment of Cotton Theory quilting
inspired me to create more designs and write this book.

Betty Cotton

Contents

Introduction 6

What is Cotton Theory Quilting? 7

Part One – Getting Ready

Supplies 9

Words to know 13

Part Two – The Basics

Preparation 17

Techniques 21

   Highway™ 21

   One-Way Street™ 22

   Aligned Intersections 23

   Quilted Embroidery 24

   Bobbin Work 24

   Boardwalk 25

   Sculptured Edges and Scalloped Borders 26

Stitches 28

   Quilting Stitches 28

   Joining Stitches 28

   Directional Stitches 28

Part Three – Cotton Theory Projects

Kitchen Trivet 30

Kitchen Placemats 34

Table Topper 39

Embroidered Table Topper 47

Cardinal Table Runner 55

Two Seasons Table Runner 62

Two-Image Tote 68

Appliquéd Wall Hanging 76

Cardinal Wall Hanging 89

Tick-Tack-Toe Quilt 90

Two Little Tots Baby Quilt 103

Two Little Tots Baby Pillow 115

Two Little Tots Bath Mat 120

Two Dear Darling Daughters Bed Quilt 127

Part Four – Finishing Up

Binding 143

French-Fold Binding 144

Bias Binding 145

Reversible Binding 146

Highway Binding 148

Sidewalk Binding 149

Introduction

Betty Cotton and her creative staff bring you
a truly unique way to quilt.
It's quilting for the 21st century.

Cotton Theory™ projects
in this book use the fast, fun and easy
Quilt First – Then Assemble™ method
of quilting along with Betty Cotton's
fold-and-finish procedures.
If you follow the instructions,
you will have a completed, reversible quilt
with a new dimension.

This book is perfect for people who have never quilted
and for those with years of experience.
You will be amazed at all of
the quilting possibilities from your sewing machine.

What is Cotton Theory™ Quilting?

Cotton Theory quilting is a new and different way to construct your quilt. It's backward!

Unlike traditional quilts, which are pieced together, layered with batting and then quilted, Cotton Theory projects are quilted first, one segment at a time, and then assembled using Betty Cotton's fold-and-finish procedures.

Contrast thread topstitching

Most quilters enjoy piecing together the top of a traditional quilt because they can see the design as it takes shape, and the results are rewarding. The actual quilting, however, can be a challenge, especially if your traditional quilt is large. Often, quilting becomes the least favorite part of constructing a quilt.

The Cotton Theory method makes quilting easy, no matter the size of your quilt. You quilt each piece individually before you construct your project, so quilting becomes just as enjoyable as piecing together a design.

Decorative stitch for quilting

You can quilt pieces creatively and accurately to produce completely reversible quilts with beautiful embroidery and bobbin work.

During Cotton Theory assembly, you sew the raw edges of your quilted pieces together, leaving seam allowances that are folded on the outside of your quilt and then stitched in place using one or more Cotton Theory techniques. This adds an extra dimension to the surface. The result is a reversible quilt that combines sewing, quilting, and embroidery. You end up with two quilts – one on each side – by constructing one project.

All work is done with a sewing machine; there's no need to do handwork.

Quilted embroidery bobbin work

It's fast, fun, and completely unique.

Part One
Getting Ready

The right sewing, quilting, and embroidery supplies
will help you achieve professional results.

Supplies

Fabric

❖ Good quality fabric is essential.

❖ Select fabrics of compatible weight for each project.

❖ Choose lightweight, 100 percent cotton fabrics for quilts and quilt-like projects.

❖ Choose medium-weight, 100 percent cotton fabrics for area rugs and floor quilts.

❖ Preshrinking is strongly recommended. Washing and drying will preshrink fabric and remove excess dye and sizing. Batting will automatically shrink with the pressing of a hot steam iron.

❖ Quilters who prefer not to prewash fabrics should expect bleeding of dyes and some shrinkage if a quilt project is washed. The decision to prewash fabrics is up to the quilter and may depend on the type of project.

Batting

Cotton Theory Batting

❖ Cotton Theory Batting is 80 percent cotton, 20 percent polyester, and is perfect for all Cotton Theory projects. Because this batting is only 18 inches wide, it fits on cutting mats. It is completely washable, has no wrinkles or creases, and has very little shrinkage (3 percent). When pressed with a hot steam iron, the 20 percent polyester in the batting lightly adheres to cotton fabrics, temporarily holding them together and eliminating pinning. The batting will become half the thickness when pressed with hot steam, giving projects drapeability. Cotton Theory Batting can be ordered on the Internet at www.quiltyard.com or by phoning (715) 597-2883 or (800) 673-8075.

Cutting Tools and Equipment

❖ **Cutting table** – A 36-inch high cutting surface is comfortable for most people to use while standing.

❖ **Rotary cutters** – Use a 45 mm cutter for lightweight fabric and a 60 mm cutter for batting. Cover the blade when the cutter is not in use.

- ❖ **Acrylic rulers** – Use a 5" x 24" ruler for fabric, a 4" x 36" ruler for batting, a 1" x 6" ruler for measuring placement of a quilting guide or seam gauge, and a 12" x 12" acrylic ruler for squaring up corners. The rulers should have ⅛-inch, ¼-inch, and 45-degree marks.

- ❖ **Self-healing cutting mat** – A 24" x 36" mat works well for fabric and batting. Markings for ⅛-inch increments and 45 degrees are helpful.

- ❖ **Scissors** – You'll need a large shears that can cut through several layers of fabric, a small thread snips to cut threads, and a seam ripper to remove stitches.

Marking Tools

- ❖ Use yellow marking chalk on dark colored fabric and blue marking chalk on light colored fabric. Test the chalk on scrap fabric to make sure it is safe to use in your project.

Sewing Tools

- ❖ **Sewing machine and accessories** – A straight stitch and zigzag stitch are required. Decorative stitches and an embroidery unit are optional.

  A ¼-inch presser foot is helpful for accurate piecing of traditional quilting. This presser foot allows you to sew ¼-inch seam allowances easily.

  A walking foot is extremely beneficial. It evenly feeds layers when you're quilting by machine.

Adhesive Quilting Guide

- ❖ **Cotton Theory Adhesive Quilting Guide** – When used on your sewing machine, this adhesive tool helps you guide the raw edges of your fabric to produce accurate quilting and precise seam allowances.

  The Cotton Theory Adhesive Quilting Guide can be ordered on the Internet at www.quiltyard.com or by calling (715) 597-2883 or (800) 673-8075. Adhesive refills for the guide also are available.

- ❖ **Straight pins and holder** – Use thin and sharp straight pins with glass heads. A magnetic straight pin holder works best to keep pins where they belong when they're not in use. If you prefer, you can use wash-away, double-sided, ¼-inch tape to eliminate pinning.

- ❖ **Machine needles** – When quilting, use size 80/12 needles for lightweight fabric and size 90/14 for medium-weight fabric. When topstitching, use size 90/14 needles for quilt projects and size 100/16 for rugs. Keep a supply of needles on hand; they will dull quickly.

- ❖ **Hand needle** – Use a sharp, No. 11 needle for tacking mitered corners of binding.

- ❖ **Thread** – You can use a variety of weights and brands in solid as well as variegated colors. Different threads will create different effects on the front side as well as the back side of your project.

  A 50-weight cotton thread works well on the top of your sewing machine as well as the bobbin for all aspects of Cotton Theory projects, including quilting, piecing, assembly, topstitching, and embroidery.

  You can use 30-weight to 40-weight cotton thread on the top and 50-weight cotton thread in the bobbin without adjusting the bobbin tension.

  Choose specialty threads, such as metallic, rayon, and some blends, if you want to change the look of your work or emphasize a certain area when quilting.

- ❖ **Cone holder** – This holds large spools or 2,000-yard to 3,000-yard cones of thread.

- ❖ **Bobbins** – Keep a minimum of 4 to 6 bobbins on hand for small projects and 10 to 12 for large projects.

- ❖ **Tape measure** – Choose one that measures 120 inches.

- ❖ **Lint brush** – A good-quality, ½-inch paint brush is ideal for cleaning the bobbin case and presser bar of your sewing machine. Use it often.

Pressing Tools

- ❖ **Iron** – For best results, use a heavyweight, self-cleaning iron that produces heavy steam and has small holes in the bottom plate.

- ❖ **Ironing board** – You'll need an ironing board or other large, padded surface to press your pieces.

- ❖ **Spring water** – Use bottled spring water to fill your iron and create steam. Spring water is free of added chemicals.

Embroidery Tools

If you plan to do quilted embroidery, you'll need the following tools:

- ❖ **Embroidery machine or a sewing machine with an embroidery unit**.

- ❖ **Embroidery designs** – Outline designs work best.

- ❖ **Embroidery needles** – Size 90/14 titanium machine embroidery needles work well.

Outline designs work best for quilted embroidery.

- ❖ **Water-soluble stabilizer** – The stabilizer helps hold fabric during machine embroidery.
- ❖ **Embroidery hoops** – A 225 mm x 140 mm hoop is recommended.
- ❖ **Thread** – You can use a variety of weights and brands.
- ❖ **Bobbins** – Do not use prewound bobbins. Fill bobbins with good-quality thread.
- ❖ **Embroidery scissors** – A 4-inch to 5-inch machine embroidery scissors is useful.

Other Tools

- ❖ **Swing-arm lamp** – This type of lamp allows you to put direct light where you want it when you are layering, pinning, quilting, sewing, folding, and topstitching.
- ❖ **Adjustable chair** – For greatest comfort and support while sewing and quilting, use a chair that's adjustable.
- ❖ **Spray sizing** – Use sizing to make ironing easier without added stiffness.
- ❖ **Sliding seam gauge** – This 6-inch ruler with a slide mechanism allows you to lock in a specific measurement.

Words to Know

Back side – When selecting fabric for a reversible quilt, this is the right side of the back fabric.

Back sides together – Placing reversible quilted pieces against each other back side to back side, with right sides of the back fabric together, when assembling a Cotton Theory quilt.

Batting – A layer of material between front-side and back-side fabrics that adds dimension and warmth to quilt projects.

Bias – The diagonal of woven fabric, generally a 45-degree angle to any straight edge. This angle provides the most stretch. (See Fabric Diagram 1.)

Bias binding – Binding made from fabric squares that have been cut on the bias and then sewn together into a long strip.

Binding – The finished edge of a quilt, consisting of a continuous strip of fabric sewn onto the back side of the quilt and then folded over to the front side, where it is sewn in place by machine.

Boardwalk – A contrast fabric strip that is added to a quilted piece. It is similar to piping or a flange, except that it is double-folded back to its original seam.

Bobbin work – The use of heavy, decorative threads, such as silk ribbon, floss, and yarn, that are too thick to fit through the eye of the sewing machine needle.

Chain quilting – Continuously feeding quilt pieces under the presser foot of a sewing machine one after the other. This speeds up quilting and creates a chain of pieces that are later separated by snipping a few threads.

Channel – The space between two parallel rows of stitching.

Channel stitching – Quilting done in a series of lines that are spaced evenly apart, creating channels.

Connector (or sashing) – The quilted piece that connects blocks, rows, or sections of a quilt.

Cotton Theory seam - A seam consisting of enlarged seam allowances folded and stitched on the outside of a Cotton Theory quilt, creating an extra dimension in the fabric.

Crosswise grain – The direction of woven fabric that runs selvage to selvage. (See Fabric Diagram 1.)

Decorative stitch – Any stitch other than a straight stitch.

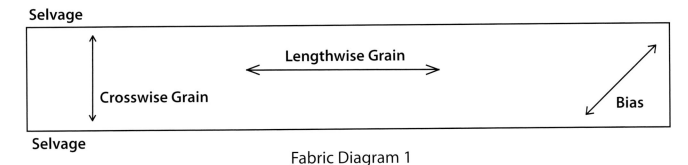

Fabric Diagram 1

Directional stitch – Any stitch that extends only in one direction, either to the right or to the left, when it is sewn. Blanket stitches and hem stitches are examples of directional stitches.

Double-fold – Folding fabric twice. Generally the fabric is folded ¼ inch from its edge and then is folded over ⅜ inch again.

Fat eighth – A quarter of a yard of fabric that is opened to its full width and cut in half parallel to the selvages. This creates an eighth of a yard that is fatter than standard. With fabric that is 42 inches wide, a fat eighth is 9" x 21", and a standard eighth is 4½" x 42".

Fat quarter – One-half yard of fabric that is opened to its full width and cut in half parallel to the selvages. This creates a quarter of a yard that is fatter than standard. With fabric that is 42 inches wide, a fat quarter is 18" x 21", and a standard quarter is 9" x 42".

Front side – When selecting fabric for a reversible quilt, this is the right side of the front fabric.

Highway™ construction – Finishing seams on the outside of a project by pressing seam allowances open and then double-folding both sides before stitching them into place. This gives the appearance of a highway that has two lanes.

Joining stitch – Any stitch that extends left and right with equal width measurements, often joining two sides. Such stitches include the zigzag, bridging stitch, feather stitch, and herringbone.

Label – Information about a quilt project and maker that is stitched to or stitched in the finished project.

Layering – Placing batting between the wrong sides of front-side fabric and back-side fabric.

Lengthwise grain – The direction of woven fabric that runs parallel to the selvage. (See Fabric Diagram 1 on Page 13.)

One-Way Street™ construction – Finishing seams on the outside of a project by pressing seam allowances all to one side, trimming the top two seam allowances, and then double-folding the remaining two seam allowances before stitching them into place. This gives the appearance of a one-way street that has only one lane.

Piecing – Joining two fabric pieces with right sides together and usually with a ¼-inch seam, unless otherwise noted.

Press – Using an iron at a cotton or linen setting to press front and back sides of projects with steam after each stage of construction for a neat and smooth finished appearance.

Presser foot width – The width between the needle and outside edge of the presser foot on a sewing machine.

Quilting – The process of sewing together at least three layers of materials.

Reversible binding – Two different fabrics pieced together lengthwise to give a reversible quilt compatible fabric binding that matches each side.

Right sides together – Placing two fabrics or fabric sections together with their brighter sides, or right sides, against each other.

Sashing (or connector) – The quilted piece that connects blocks, rows, or sections of a quilt.

Scrappy – A mixture of colors and prints with no prearranged order.

Seam allowance – The distance between cut edges of fabric and the seam. The seam allowance is created by stitching together two pieces. The allowance usually is ¼ inch from the cut edge for traditional piecing and 1 inch or more from the cut edge for Cotton Theory projects.

Selvage – The manufactured, tightly woven, narrow edge of fabric that prevents the cloth from raveling. Selvage edges should be removed and should not be used in quilt projects.

Sidewalk binding – A strip of fabric added around the edge of a quilt before applying the actual binding. This strip looks like a path, or sidewalk, adjacent to the binding.

Stitch in the ditch – To stitch on an existing seam line.

Stitch length – The distance between stitch links, measured in a metric scale. The higher the number, the longer the stitch. A stitch length of 3.5 is ideal for quilting and assembly.

Stitch width – The distance from one side of a stitch to the other side. The higher the number, the wider the stitch.

Strip – A piece of fabric cut from selvage to selvage (crosswise grain). (See Fabric Diagram 2.)

Sub-cut – A second cut (lengthwise grain) taken from the original cut strip. (See Fabric Diagram 3.)

Tension – The interlocking of the top thread and bobbin thread on a sewing machine. With the correct tension, thread should interlock midway between fabric layers so that stitches lie flat and fabric does not pucker.

Topstitching – Functional or decorative stitching sewn over a fold or seam.

Wrong side – The dull side, or inside surface, of fabric. Usually this side is not intended to be seen in a completed project.

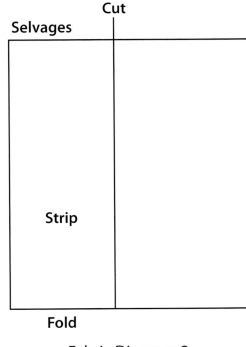

Fabric Diagram 2

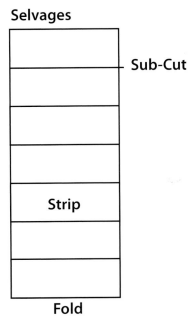

Fabric Diagram 3

Part Two
The Basics

These layered pieces are ready for quilting.

Preparation

Fabric Selection

Cotton Theory quilting is backward from traditional quilting. A typical quilt has a pieced top and usually one fabric for the back. But Cotton Theory quilts are automatically reversible when completed. The back-side fabric is also cut into pieces, so you need fabrics and identical yardage for both sides of the quilt.

Following is some advice for selecting front-side and back-side fabrics.

For easy selection:

❖ Use a different color theme on each side of your project. For instance, use pink fabrics on one side and blues on the other.

All Cotton Theory projects are completely reversible.

❖ Pair up front-side dark fabrics with back-side dark fabrics and front-side light fabrics with back-side light fabrics.

❖ Use prints of similar scale for each side. For example, use large floral prints on both sides or small floral prints on both sides.

These steps will give you a quilt with identical pieces, but different color themes, on each side.

For advanced selection:

❖ Choose front-side and back-side fabrics that are very different in color and scale, creating a different look on each side. For example, on the front side you could have a carefully prearranged color scheme, and on the back side you could have a scrappy look that has a mixture of colors and prints with no prearranged order. This type of advanced fabric selection requires practice.

Prearranged design

Scrappy design

Thread selection

The fabric decides how you do the quilting and what thread you choose. In a typical quilt, the thread usually matches or blends with the back-side fabric. But because Cotton Theory quilts are reversible, you need to choose threads for both sides of the quilt. You can have one color of thread in your bobbin and a totally different color in the top part of your sewing machine.

❖ For busy prints, match the thread to your fabric, and use simple, straight-line quilting stitches.

❖ For simple prints and plain fabrics, choose a contrast thread color and use decorative stitches to add appealing details to your quilt.

Cutting

Cutting is another aspect of Cotton Theory quilting that differs from traditional quilting.

When working with small pieces of fabric, cut front-side and back-side pieces together. This eliminates pairing them up later. When you're ready to start quilting, all you have to do is insert batting pieces that have been cut to the correct size.

Label your cut pieces to avoid confusion during construction of your project.

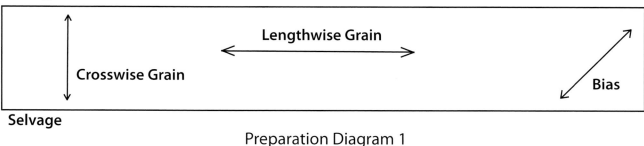

Preparation Diagram 1

Remember that the lengthwise grain is stronger than the crosswise grain of fabric. (See Preparation Diagram 1.) Whenever possible, folded seam allowances in your project should be the lengthwise grain. This will make the fabric cooperate better, with little or no stretching, and your quilted pieces should remain their true size.

Example: Cut one 6-inch strip (selvage to selvage), and then sub-cut eight 4" x 6" strips (cut from the first strip). (See Preparation Diagrams 2 and 3.)

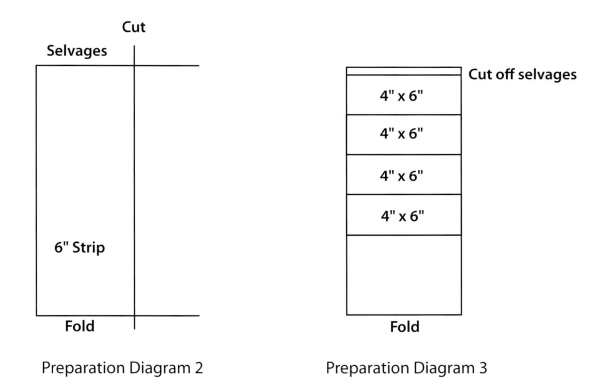

Preparation Diagram 2   Preparation Diagram 3

Layering

Batting is a very important part of Cotton Theory quilting. Like fabric, it too is cut piece by piece for construction. The batting turns your cut fabric pieces into a quilt.

When selecting batting, consider factors such as weight, warmth, loft, shrinkage, washability, size, and the way it drapes.

Cotton Theory Batting, available at www.quiltyard.com, is 80 percent cotton and 20 percent polyester. It has very little shrinkage, is completely washable, and will hold up to a hot steam iron without melting. It becomes a low-loft batting after pressing, but when tumbled in the dryer, the loft returns and the dimensions in your quilt become more noticeable. The small amount of polyester in the batting temporarily fuses cotton fabric layers together when pressed, eliminating pinning in most cases. The batting comes in 18-inch widths to make cutting easier, and it has no creases or wrinkles.

In Cotton Theory projects, batting has its own piece-by-piece cutting instructions. The batting is not included in the seam allowances of fabrics.

Preparation Diagram 4 shows basic layering of fabrics and batting in Cotton Theory projects.

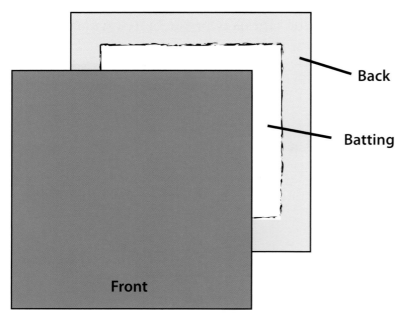

Preparation Diagram 4

Techniques

With Cotton Theory techniques, one quilted piece is sewn to another quilted piece, and a minimum 1-inch seam allowance is used. The enlarged seam allowance is finished on the outside of the quilt, adding an extra decorative dimension.

Batting is cut smaller than fabric pieces and is not part of the seam allowance, because this would cause too much bulk in the seams. The batting, which measures 1 inch less than the fabric on all sides, is layered between two fabric pieces and is quilted in place, leaving raw edges that are finished into a reversible quilt.

Cotton Theory techniques include Highway™ and One-Way Street™ fold-and-finish procedures, a construction method called Aligned Intersections, various quilted embroidery and bobbin work, and decorative accents such as a Boardwalk flange, sculptured edges, and scalloped borders.

The Highway™

The Highway is a great way to attach one quilted piece to another if you won't be crossing over bulky seams. For bulky seamed pieces, use the One-Way Street procedure (Page 22).

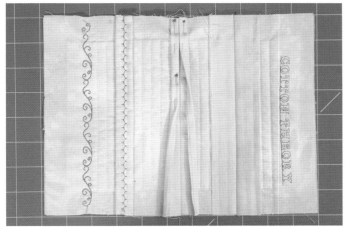

This photo shows various stages of the Highway procedure. First, seams are pressed open; then they are double-folded and pinned; and then they are stitched.

With the Highway procedure, two quilted pieces are sewn together, and then seam allowances are pressed open, with two layers of fabric on each side of the seam. (Cotton Theory seam allowances have a total of four layers of fabric — two from each quilted piece.) Because of the extra layers, it's best to press both sides of the project to ensure that seams are completely open and lie flat. Use a steam iron to press seams open on one side; then flip the project over and press the other side.

Betty's Advice: *Replace straight pins regularly. They become dull.*

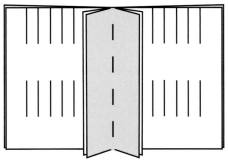

To finish a seam:

❖ Double-fold each side of the seam allowance (two layers) toward the center, and pin it in place. To accomplish this, fold each side ¼ inch and then fold it again so it meets the seam line in the middle. Raw edges of the fabric are now tucked inside the folds. All pins should face the same direction so they can be removed easily while topstitching. If you prefer, you can eliminate pinning by using wash-away, double-sided, ¼-inch tape.

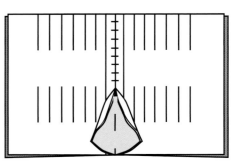

❖ Topstitch across the center line where the two sides meet. The stitch should be wide enough to sew both sides of the folded seam allowances at the same time. Topstitch through all layers. (See Stitches on Page 28 for advice on choosing stitches.)

One-Way Street™

The One-Way Street technique has more flexibility than the Highway. It allows you to cross over a previously folded and stitched seam.

After two quilted pieces are sewn together, the seam allowances are pressed in one direction, with the four layers of fabric on one side. (Cotton Theory seam allowances have four layers — two from each quilted piece.)

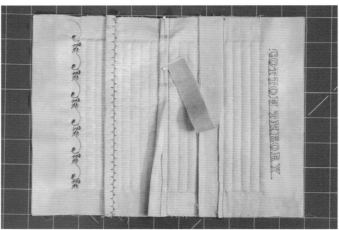

This photo shows stages of the One-Way Street procedure. First, seams are pressed to one side and the top two layers are trimmed; then the remaining two layers are double-folded and pinned; and lastly the fold is stitched.

To finish a seam:

❖ Press all seam allowances to one side (total of four on one side). To ensure that seams are smooth and flat, use a steam iron to press the opposite side of the project first; then press the side that has seam allowances.

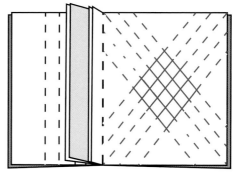

❖ Trim the top two layers of the seam allowances to ¼ inch. Do not cut the bottom two layers because these will be needed for folding and finishing.

❖ Double-fold the remaining seam allowance layers back to the line where the seam was stitched (not past it), and pin the fold in place. To accomplish this, make a ¼-inch fold and then fold it again to the seam line. Raw edges of the fabric are now tucked inside the folds. Do not cover up the original seam line while folding; you need to barely see it when you are topstitching. To make sewing and pin removal easier, position the fabric so you fold seam allowances toward you if you pin fabric right-handed or away from you if you pin fabric left-handed. This will put straight pins in the proper direction for easy removal, and as the project gets larger, bulk will not build up in the

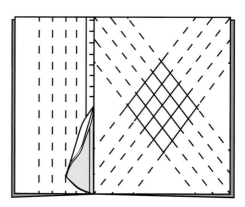

throat of the sewing machine. If you prefer, you can eliminate pinning by using wash-away, double-sided, ¼-inch tape.

❖ Using a zigzag or decorative stitch of your choice, topstitch the folded fabric in place. To do this, stitch in the ditch (on the previous seam line), going on and off the fold. (See Stitches on Page 28 for advice on choosing stitches.)

Crossing over a seam:

The One-Way Street is the technique to use when attaching one quilted piece to another that already has a folded and finished seam.

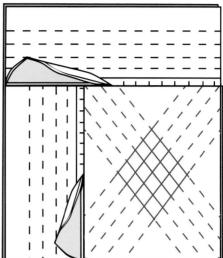

Follow the previous instructions for finishing a One-Way Street seam, but keep these points in mind:

❖ Trim the old, and fold the new. In other words, press seam allowances to one side so that the intersecting seam you will be sewing across is on top. Then trim the top two seam allowance layers (the old seam) to ¼ inch or less to reduce the fabric bulk.

❖ After trimming, double-fold the remaining seam allowances and topstitch by following the previous directions for the One-Way Street technique.

Aligned Intersections

When connecting sections of a quilted project, it's important to line up the seams of quilted strips to achieve a professionally finished look. This is called aligning the intersections. Even though connectors, or sashings, are used, and the intersections do not actually intersect, they do need to be aligned.

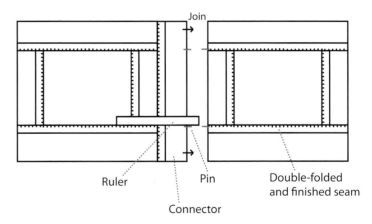

Follow these steps:

❖ Sew, fold, and finish one side of the connector.

❖ Place a ruler along the previously finished seam.

❖ Place a pin in the raw edges of the connector to mark the spot that lines up with the seam.

❖ Align the pin with the previously finished seam on the block you are connecting.

❖ Sew the quilted pieces together.

A bulky seam should not join with another bulky seam, so it's necessary to use a connector, or sashing, to assemble Cotton Theory projects.

Quilted Embroidery

Machine embroidery designs can be used to quilt pieces of Cotton Theory projects. You simply place all three layers — back-side fabric, batting and front-side fabric — in or on an embroidery hoop and embroider as usual. Select good-quality thread, and choose thread colors for the back side as well as the front side of the embroidery, because the finished project will be reversible.

When choosing embroidery designs, look for ones that are outlines or are not very full (less dense). Avoid wide satin-stitch outlines because it is difficult to lock the tension exactly in the middle on these. You may be able to disguise imperfect tension with your thread choices. Variegated threads are great ones to use in the upper part of the sewing machine and in the bobbin.

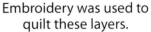

Embroidery was used to quilt these layers.

It may be necessary to raise the upper tension on the sewing machine. Rayon 40-weight threads usually need a looser upper tension of 2.0 to 2.5 mm (metric scale.) Cotton 50-weight threads usually need a tighter upper tension of 3.0 to 3.5 mm.

It's a good idea to do a practice piece first when embroidering.

Add the fabric and batting layers to your machine hoop in one of two ways:

❖ If layers are large enough to stay tight in the hoop, you do not need to use a layer of water-soluble stabilizer, because the batting will act as a stabilizer. Cutting fabric and batting pieces larger when you plan to embroider them may be helpful. However, you will need to trim the fabric and batting to the correct size later.

❖ If pieces are too small to stay in the hoop tightly, put a layer of water-soluble stabilizer in the hoop, and place your layered pieces on top of the stabilizer. Baste the layers and stabilizer in place, and then embroider the design. Remove the basting and wash away the stabilizer after embroidering.

Bobbin Work

You can feature bobbin work on the front side of projects by placing layers on your machine embroidery hoop upside down (back-side fabric up).

With bobbin work, thread choices are important. Here's some advice:

❖ Because it's almost impossible to lock the sewing machine's tension in the middle of the quilt layers, the top thread usually will appear on the back side of the layers as tiny dots. This can be very noticeable when there is a strong contrast in thread colors on top and in the bobbin. If possible, top and bobbin threads should blend together when doing bobbin work so that your finished bobbin embroidery is sharp and clear.

Bobbin work can be a decorative addition to your project.

❖ Wind bobbins about ¾ full. The thickness of thread will vary. You can wind bobbins by machine, but you may have to bypass the thread guide.

❖ To determine how much thread is on the bobbin, first wind the bobbin; then take the thread off the bobbin, measure the yardage, and wind it back on the bobbin. After stitching an embroidery design, measure the amount remaining on the bobbin.

❖ Heavy threads that are too large to fit through the eye of a sewing machine needle can be machine-wound on the bobbin and used for all aspects of Cotton Theory quilting, from straight-line quilting to decorative quilting to topstitching to embroidery. Heavy threads are ideal for embroidery outlines (running stitch) and for loose, light, and airy decorative stitches. Avoid wide satin stitches and dense fill-ins. It's a good idea to invest in a second bobbin case for heavier threads and to mark it with nail polish to identify it easily.

❖ On many sewing machines, adjusting the bobbin tension requires a small, regular flat-head screwdriver. Turning the screw to the left loosens the tension. Adjust the screw in very small increments and test how the machine sews. For example, using 2 mm silk ribbon in the bobbin usually requires ¼ turn to the left, and using 39 g yarn in the bobbin usually requires ½ turn to the left.

❖ When working with heavy threads, begin and end with tiny stitches (straight stitch 0.5 mm long). Avoid the .00 mm length, because you will end up stitching in place, and this will be noticeable.

Boardwalk

A Boardwalk is a contrast fabric strip added to a quilted piece. It's similar to piping or a flange, but it is double-folded back to its original seam. The Boardwalk will give you the appearance of a Cotton Theory Highway seam when stitched in place.

To construct a Boardwalk, do the following:

1. With right sides together, piece together 3" flange strips with mitered seams (45-degree angle), as shown in diagram.

2. Stitch a diagonal line across the two strips.

3. Trim the excess to ¼".

4. Press the seams open.

5. Fold the flange in half lengthwise and press.

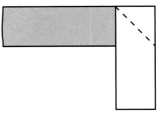

Note: Apply flange to side edges first, and then add to top and bottom.

6. Place raw edges of flange ½" from raw edges of front side of quilt.

7. Machine baste a scant 1" from raw edge of quilt.

Raw edge of quilt

Raw edge of flange

Front side of quilt

Folded edge of flange

1/2"

8. Double-fold the ends only back to the original seam (fold ¼" and fold again).

Front Side of Quilt

9. Machine baste these ends in place.

Note: Do not double-fold the entire flange. It will be double-folded later during the construction of your project.

10. Apply top and bottom flange in the same manner.

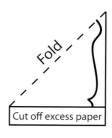

Front Side of Quilt

11. Double-fold the ends only back to the original seam, as shown in diagram, and machine-baste ends in place.

12. Continue with the rest of your project, finishing the Boardwalk using the Highway procedure when you add the next piece.

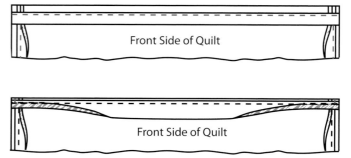

Front Side of Quilt

Sculptured Edges and Scalloped Borders

Designing sculptured edges and corners is quite easy. Freezer paper works well for making a paper pattern to use when cutting curves. If you have ever folded paper and cut paper snowflakes, then you can cut a sculptured edge for your quilt.

Fold una

Cut off excess paper

Fold a piece of freezer paper diagonally, cut off the excess to make it square and cut a few curves, as shown in diagram. (The size of the paper doesn't matter at this point.) Open your paper and you will be amazed at the sculptured lines you have created.

Cut several designs and decide which one looks best for your quilt.

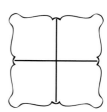

To see the entire design of your choice, cut four copies and tape them together, as shown in diagram. It's that easy.

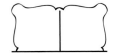

If your quilt is longer than it is wide, cut your design in half and lengthen it.

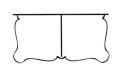

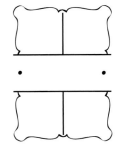

Place a dot in the center of the space you need to fill; then draw a curve from the dot to your sculptured edge.

Draw a mirror image of this curve in the opposite direction to connect to the other end of the sculptured edge.

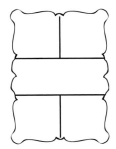

To transfer this design to your quilt edge:

- ❖ Divide your sculptured edge into four equal sections.
- ❖ Measure half of your quilt's border width and mark off four equal sections.
- ❖ Determine the ratio of your scalloped-edge drawing. For example, 1" of paper may equal 11" of quilt.
- ❖ Redraw your scalloped edge to scale.
- ❖ When cutting the scalloped edge on your quilt, remember there is no batting in the raw edges of Cotton Theory projects. Cut your sculptured edge 1" inch from the raw edges so that batting is included in the curves.

Stitches

Quilting Stitches

You can quilt layered pieces with any stitches you have in your sewing machine. However, bobbin tension may need to be adjusted if you choose dense and tight decorative stitches along with heavier threads.

It's best to select quilting stitches that are light and not too dense. The tighter the stitch, the more the quilted pieces will tighten and draw up.

Width and length measurements of stitches mentioned in this book are given in a metric scale, such as 3.5 mm.

The photo below shows stitch suggestions for quilting.

Quilting stitches

Joining Stitches

Joining stitches are used for topstitching. It is important that these stitches remain light and airy so your quilt remains soft and easy to drape.

When topstitching, it may be necessary to lengthen and widen stitches to meet the needs of your project.

The photo at the top of the next column shows some possibilities for topstitching the folds of the Highway and One-Way Street fold-and-finish procedures described in Techniques, Pages 21-23.

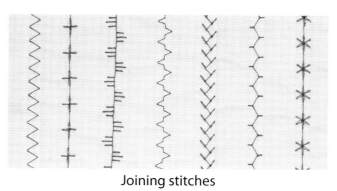

Joining stitches

Directional Stitches

You can use directional stitches to topstitch the folds for the One-Way Street procedure. However, it is important you stitch left to right, as shown in the photo below. This way, the bulk of the quilt will go to the left of the sewing machine and won't build up in the throat of the machine.

It will take practice to use directional stitches, because when you stitch in the ditch (on an existing seam), you need to be positioned exactly on the previous seam or the stitching will be obvious on the back side of your project.

If your sewing machine has a mirror-image feature for stitches, be sure the direction is set to the right, as shown in the photo below. If your stitches don't extend to the right as these do, please don't use them for Cotton Theory projects.

This photo shows several directional stitches.

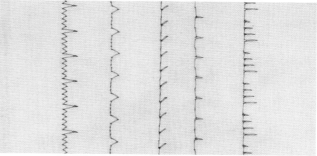

Directional stitches

Part Three
Cotton Theory Projects

Cotton Theory projects such as these placemats, table topper, and trivet are fun to make and useful, too. The following pages give instructions for 13 different projects. You can make placemats, table runners, wall hangings, throws, totes, baby quilts, bed quilts, and more.

Kitchen Trivet
(8"x 8")

Betty's Advice: *This project is great for using scraps. If you prefer not to use scraps, the yardage given for the front side is enough for both sides.*

Back side

Front side

Yardage Requirements

(Based on 42-inch wide fabric)

Front Side

Center square:	¼ yd. novelty print
Triangles:	⅛ yd. red print
Rectangles 1 & 2:	⅛ yd. tan micro check
Rectangles 3 & 4:	⅛ yd. tan/blue stripe

Binding

⅛ yd. black/tan micro check

Back Side

Use scraps of your choice

Center square:	¼ yd. large scale print
Triangles:	⅛ yd. red print
Rectangle 1:	⅛ yd. pink print
Rectangle 2:	⅛ yd. green print
Rectangle 3:	⅛ yd. gold print
Rectangle 4:	⅛ yd. second green print

Batting

Scraps of batting or a piece of Cotton Theory Batting measuring 8" x 18"

Fabric Cutting Instructions

Cut carefully, and label your cut pieces for each side of your project. Cut strips on the crosswise grain of 42-inch wide fabric. (See Fabric Diagram 2 on Page 15.)

Betty's Advice: Cut front-side and back-side fabrics together. This eliminates pairing them up later.

Front Side

Center square:
Cut 1– 8" strip
Sub-cut 1– 8" x 8"

Triangles:
Cut 1– 4" strip
Sub-cut 2– 4" x 4"

Rectangles 1 & 2:
Cut 1– 3" strip
Sub-cut 2– 3" x 8"

Rectangles 3 & 4:
Cut 1– 3" strip
Sub-cut 2– 3" x 10"

Back Side

Center square:
Cut 1– 8" strip
Sub-cut 1– 8" x 8"
(Sub-cuts are second cuts from the previous strip. See Fabric Diagram 3 on Page 15.)

Triangles:
Cut 1– 4" strip
Sub-cut 2– 4" x 4"

Rectangle 1:
Cut 1– 3" strip
Sub-cut 1– 3" x 8"

Rectangle 2:
Cut 1– 3" strip
Sub-cut 1– 3" x 8"

Rectangle 3:
Cut 1– 3" strip
Sub-cut 1– 3" x 10"

Rectangle 4:
Cut 1– 3" strip
Sub-cut 1– 3" x 10"

Binding
Cut 1– 2½" strip

Batting Cutting Instructions

Label your cut pieces.

Note: For this project, the center square will have a double layer of batting.

Center square:
Cut 2– 6" x 6"

Rectangle 1:
Cut 1– 1" x 6"

Rectangle 2:
Cut 1– 1" x 6"

Rectangle 3:
Cut 1– 1" x 8"

Rectangle 4:
Cut 1– 1" x 8"

X denotes batting that is not used

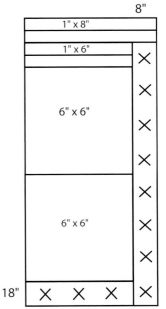

Cutting Diagram for Cotton Theory Batting (8" x 18")

Quilting Instructions

Insert quilting needle into your sewing machine. For best results, use a walking foot or even-feed foot when quilting.

Stitch suggestion: A zigzag 0.5 mm wide and 3.0 mm long will give the appearance of hand quilting, looking a little wobbly.

Thread suggestion: Match thread to the fabric for each side.

Center Square:

Optional: To make this trivet more heat resistant, add a layer of Iron Quick Teflon on each side of the batting, and eliminate one layer of batting.

1. Layer fabric and batting. With back fabric right-side down, place two layers of batting in center, and place front fabric right side up.

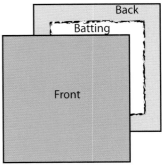

2. Press layers together with steam.

3. Place Adhesive Quilting Guide 4" to the right of sewing machine needle to guide fabric and provide straight quilting.

4. Quilt down the middle of the square.

5. Channel-stitch another row one presser-foot width away from the previous quilting (about ⅜").

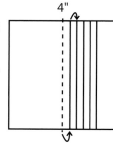

6. Repeat rows of channel stitching to within 1⅜" from edge of fabric, alternating directions to compensate for fabric shifting.

Note: Because presser-foot widths vary, the number of quilting rows will vary.

7. Channel-stitch the other half of the square in the same manner.

8. Rotate the square one half turn.

9. Repeat steps 3 through 7 to create a grid of quilting.

Front-Side Triangles:

Stitch suggestion: Use a 3.5 mm length straight stitch.

1. Mark a diagonal line on wrong sides of 4" squares.

2. With right sides together, place one 4" square on top of quilted center square so that outside edges line up and diagonal line extends across one corner of center square.

3. Stitch on the diagonal line, through all layers.

4. Trim the 4" square ¼" from the diagonal line. (Do not cut quilted center square.)

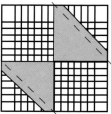

5. Repeat steps 2 through 4, placing second 4" square in opposite corner of quilted center square.

6. Press triangles toward corners, so that right side of fabric is seen.

Back-Side Triangles:

1. Mark a diagonal line on wrong sides of 4" squares.

2. With right sides together, place 4" squares on top of back-side center square in opposite corners from front side.

3. Stitch on the diagonal lines, through all layers.

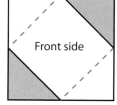

4. Trim 4" squares ¼" from the diagonal lines. (Do not cut quilted center square.)

5. Press triangles toward corners, so that right side of fabric is seen.

Red dotted lines indicate placement of 4" squares for back side.

Rectangles 1 through 4:

1. Pair up front-side and back-side rectangles.

2. Layer fabric and batting. With back fabric right-side down, place one layer of batting in center and place front fabric right side up.

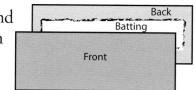

3. Press layers together with steam.

4. Place Adhesive Quilting Guide 1⅜" to the right of sewing machine needle.

5. Quilt down each side of the rectangles (total of two rows per rectangle).

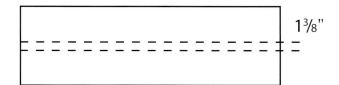

1⅜"

Assembly Instructions

Insert topstitch needle into your sewing machine. Seam allowances will be finished on the front side of the project using Highway and One-Way Street procedures.

Note: Use a 1" seam allowance when sewing your quilted pieces together.

Thread suggestion: Red 50-weight cotton on top and brown 50-weight cotton in bobbin.

1. With back sides together, sew Rectangle 1 to right-hand side of center square and Rectangle 2 to left-hand side of center square. Sew through all fabric layers.

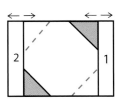

2. Press seams open on front side; then press the back side.

3. Finish seams using the Highway procedure. (See Techniques, Page 21.)

4. With back sides together, sew Rectangle 3 to bottom of center square and Rectangle 4 to top of center square. Sew through all fabric layers.

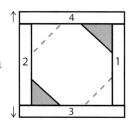

5. Press the back side; then press all seam allowances on front side toward the outside edges.

6. Finish seams using the One-Way Street procedure. (See Techniques, Pages 22.)

Betty's Advice: To ensure that seam allowances are completely flat, press both sides of your project.

Applying Binding:

1. Trim ⅝" from raw edges of project, leaving a ⅜" seam allowance on all sides.

2. Apply the binding. (For instructions, see Binding section at end of this book.)

Kitchen Placemats
Set of Four (12" x 18" each)

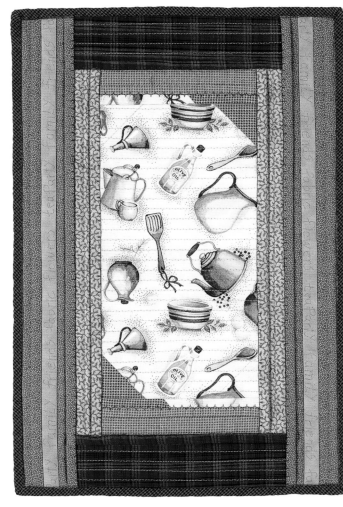

Front side of placemat

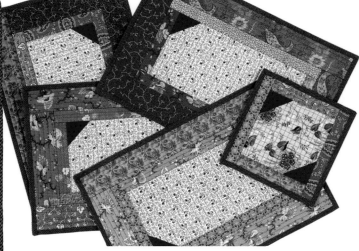

Back sides of placemats and matching trivet

Yardage Requirements

(Based on 42-inch wide fabric)

Front Side

Fabric is for four identical front sides.

Center rectangle: ½ yd. novelty print
Triangles: ⅛ yd. red micro check
Rectangles 1 & 2: ¼ yd. tan micro check
Rectangles 3 & 4: ½ yd. med. blue print
Rectangles 5 & 6: ⅜ yd. dark red plaid
Rectangles 7 & 8: ⅝ yd. tan/blue stripe

Back Side

This side is meant to be scrappy. Fabric is for four back sides that differ from one another.

Center rectangle: ½ yd. small beige print
Triangles: ⅛ yd. dark red print
Rectangles 1 & 3: ⅛ yd. each red, pink, green, blue (small prints)
Rectangles 2 & 4: ⅛ yd. each gold, brown, blue, green (small prints)
Rectangles 5 & 7: ⅛ yd. each red, pink, green, blue (large prints)
Rectangles 6 & 8: ⅛ yd. each gold, brown, blue, green (large prints)

Binding

⅝ yd. black/tan micro check

Batting

Cotton Theory Batting, 18" x 52"

Fabric Cutting Instructions

Cut carefully to ensure you have an adequate amount of fabric. Label your cut pieces for each side. Cut strips on the crosswise grain of 42-inch wide fabric. (See Fabric Diagram 2 on Page 15.)

Front Side

Center rectangle:
Cut 2– 8" strips
Sub-cut 4– 8½x 14"½
(Sub-cuts are second cuts from the previous strips. See Fabric Diagram 3, Page 15.)

Triangles:
Cut 1– 4" strip
Sub-cut 8– 4" x 4"

Rectangles 1 & 2:
Cut 1– 8" strip
Sub-cut 8– 3" x 8"

Rectangles 3 & 4:
Cut 1– 16" strip
Sub-cut 8– 3" x 16"

Rectangles 5 & 6:
Cut 1– 10" strip
Sub-cut 8– 4" x 10"

Rectangles 7 & 8:
Cut 1– 20" strip
Sub-cut 8– 4" x 20"

Back Side

Center rectangle:
Cut 2– 8" strips
Sub-cut 4– 8" x 14"

Triangles:
Cut 1– 4" strip
Sub-cut 8– 4" x 4"

From red, pink, green, blue small prints:
Cut 1 each 3" strip (total of 4 strips)

Rectangle 1:
Sub-cut 1 each 3" x 8" (total of 4)

Rectangle 3:
Sub-cut 1 each 3" x 16" (total of 4)

From gold, brown, blue, green small prints:
Cut 1 each 3" strip (total of 4 strips)

Rectangle 2:
Sub-cut 1 each 3" x 8" (total of 4)

Rectangle 4:
Sub-cut 1 each 3" x 16" (total of 4)

From red, pink, green, blue large prints:
Cut 1 each 4" strip (total of 4 strips)

Rectangle 5:
Sub-cut 1 each 4" x 10" (total of 4)

Rectangle 7:
Sub-cut 1 each 4" x 20" (total of 4)

From gold, brown, blue, green large prints:
Cut 1 each 4" strip (total of 4 strips)

Rectangle 6:
Sub-cut 1 each 4" x 10" (total of 4)

Rectangle 8:
Sub-cut 1 each 4" x 20" (total of 4)

Bias Binding
Cut 2– 20" x 20" squares

Batting Cutting Instructions

Label your cut pieces.

Center rectangle:
Cut 4– 6"x 12"

Rectangle 1:
Cut 4– 1" x 6"

Rectangle 2:
Cut 4– 1" x 6"

Rectangle 3:
Cut 4– 1" x 14"

Rectangle 4:
Cut 4– 1" x 14"

Rectangle 5:
Cut 4– 2" x 8"

Rectangle 6:
Cut 4– 2" x 8"

Rectangle 7:
Cut 4– 2" x 18"

Rectangle 8:
Cut 4– 2" x 18"

X denotes batting that is not used

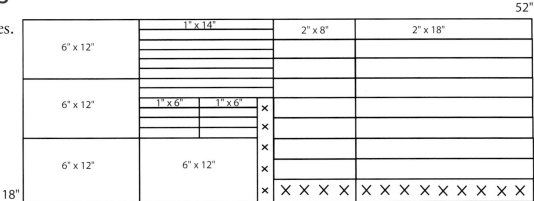

Cutting Diagram for Cotton Theory Batting (18" x 52")

Quilting Instructions

Insert quilting needle into your sewing machine. For best results, use a walking foot or even-feed foot when quilting.

Stitch suggestion: A zigzag 0.5 mm wide and 3.0 mm long will give the appearance of hand quilting, looking a little wobbly.

Thread suggestion: Match thread to the fabric for each side.

Center Rectangle:

1. Layer fabric and batting. With back fabric right-side down, place batting in center and place front fabric right side up.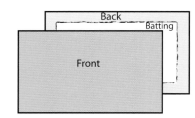

2. Press layers together with steam.

3. Mark a vertical line 7" from one of the short sides of the rectangle. This is the middle of the rectangle.

4. Quilt down the middle.

5. Channel-stitch another row one presser-foot width away from the previous quilting.

6. Repeat rows of channel stitching to within 1⅜" from edge of fabric, alternating directions to compensate for any fabric shifting.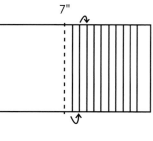

Note: Because presser-foot widths vary, the number of quilting rows will vary.

7. Channel-stitch the other half of the rectangle in the same manner.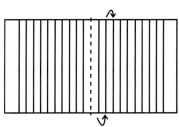

Front-Side Triangles:

Stitch suggestion: Use a 3.5 mm length straight stitch.

1. Mark a diagonal line on wrong sides of 4" squares.

2. With right sides together, place 4" squares on top of quilted center rectangle so that outside edges line up and diagonal lines extend across corners of center rectangle.

3. Stitch on the diagonal lines, through all layers.

4. Trim the 4" squares ¼" from the diagonal lines, as shown in diagram. (Do not cut quilted center rectangle.)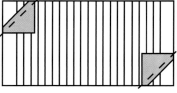

5. Press triangles toward corners, so that right side of fabric is seen.

Back-Side Triangles:

1. Mark a diagonal line on wrong sides of 4" squares.

2. With right sides together, place 4" squares on top of back-side center rectangle in opposite corners from front side.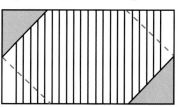

Red dotted lines indicate placement of 4" squares for back side.

3. Stitch on the diagonal lines, through all layers.

4. Trim the 4" squares ¼" from the diagonal lines. (Do not cut quilted center rectangle.)

5. Press triangles toward corners, so that right side of fabric is seen.

Rectangles 1 through 4:

1. Pair up front-side and back-side rectangles 1 through 4.

2. Layer fabric and batting. With back fabric right-side down, place 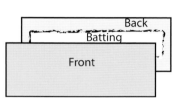 one layer of batting in center and place front fabric right side up.

3. Press layers together with steam.

4. Place Adhesive Quilting Guide 1⅜" to the right of sewing machine needle.

5. Quilt down each side of the rectangles (total of two rows per rectangle).

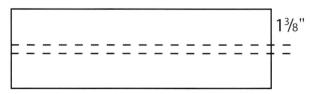

Rectangles 5 through 8:

1. Pair up front-side and back-side rectangles 5 through 8.

2. Layer fabric and batting. With back fabric right-side down, place one layer of batting in center and place front fabric right side up.

3. Press layers together with steam.

4. Place Adhesive Quilting Guide 2" to the right of sewing machine needle.

5. Quilt down the middle of each rectangle.

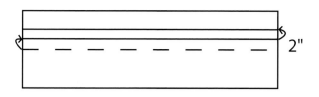

6. Channel-stitch another row one presser-foot width away from the previous quilting.

7. Reverse directions, and channel-stitch an additional row one presser-foot width away from the previous quilting.

8. Channel-stitch the other half of the rectangle in the same manner (total of five rows).

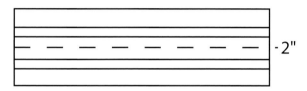

Assembly Instructions

Insert topstitch needle into your sewing machine. Seam allowances will be finished on the front side using Highway and One-Way Street procedures.

Note: Use a 1" seam allowance when sewing your quilted pieces together.

Thread suggestion: Red 50-weight cotton on top and brown 50-weight cotton in bobbin.

1. With back sides together, use a 3.5 mm length straight stitch to sew Rectangle 1 to right-hand side of center rectangle and to sew Rectangle 2 to left-hand side of center rectangle. Sew through all fabric layers.

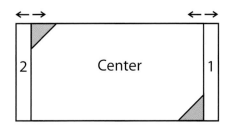

2. Press seams open on front side; then press the back side.

3. Finish seams using the Highway procedure. (See Techniques, Page 21.)

4. With back sides together, sew Rectangle 3 (same back-side fabric as Rectangle 1) to bottom of center rectangle and sew Rectangle 4 (same fabric as Rectangle 2) to top of center rectangle. Sew through all fabric layers.

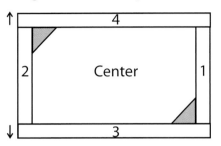

5. Press the back side; then press all seam allowances on front side toward the outside edges.

6. Finish seams using the One-Way Street procedure. (See Techniques, Page 22.)

7. With back sides together, sew Rectangle 5 (same color family as Rectangle 1) to right-hand side of project and sew Rectangle 6 (same color family as Rectangle 2) to left-hand side.

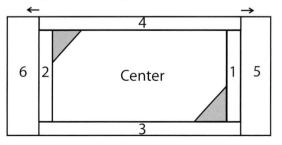

8. Press the back side; then press all seam allowances on front side toward the outside edges.

9. Finish seams using the One-Way Street procedure.

10. With back sides together, sew Rectangle 7 (same fabric as Rectangle 5) to bottom of project and sew Rectangle 8 (same fabric as Rectangle 6) to top.

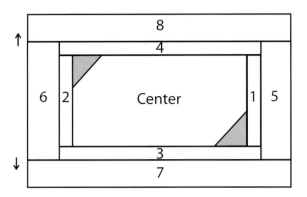

11. Press the back side; then press all seam allowances on front side toward the outside edges.

12. Finish seams using the One-Way Street procedure.

Applying Binding:

1. Trim ⅝" from raw edges of project, leaving a ⅜" seam allowance on all sides.

2. Apply bias binding. (For instructions, see Binding section at end of this book.)

Table Topper
(23" x 23")

Front side of Table Topper

Back side of Table Topper

Yardage Requirements

(Based on 42-inch wide fabric)

Front Side

Center square:	¼ yd. novelty print
Triangles:	⅛ yd. red micro check
Rectangles 1 & 3:	⅜ yd. med. blue print
Rectangles 2 & 4:	⅜ yd. red plaid
Borders 5 & 6:	½ yd. tan micro check
Sashings 7 & 8:	¼ yd. blue print

(Sashings connect sections of a quilt.)

Binding

¼ yd. black/tan micro check

Back Side

This side is meant to look scrappy.

Center square:	¼ yd. small beige print
Triangles:	⅛ yd. dark brown print
Rectangles 1 & 3:	⅛ yd. each of 4 assorted blue prints
Rectangle 2:	⅛ yd. each red, pink, green, gold prints
Rectangle 4:	⅛ yd. each different red, pink, green, gold prints
Borders 5 & 6:	½ yd. large beige print
Sashings 7 & 8:	⅛ yd. each of 3 more assorted blue prints

Batting

Cotton Theory Batting, 18" x 37"

Fabric Cutting Instructions

Cut carefully to ensure you have an adequate amount of fabric. Label your cut pieces for each side. Cut strips on the crosswise grain of 42-inch wide fabric. (See Fabric Diagram 2 on Page 15.)

Front Side

Center square:
Cut 1– 8" strip
Sub-cut 4 – 8" x 8"
(Sub-cuts are second cuts from the previous strips. See Fabric Diagram 3 on Page 15.)

Triangles:
Cut 1– 4" strip
Sub-cut 8– 4" x 4"

From medium blue print:
Cut 1– 10" strip
Rectangle 3:
Sub-cut 4– 3" x 10"
Rectangle 1:
Sub-cut 4– 3" x 8"

From red plaid:
Cut 1– 10" strip
Rectangle 4:
Sub-cut 4– 3" x 10"

Rectangle 2:
Sub-cut 4– 3" x 8"

Borders 5 & 6:
Cut 1– 13" strip
Sub-cut 4– 5" x 13"
Sub-cut 4– 5" x 10"

Sashings 7 & 8:
Cut 2– 3" strips
Sub-cut 1– 3" x 25"
Sub-cut 2– 3" x 13"

Back Side

Center square:
Cut 1– 8" strip
Sub-cut 4 – 8" x 8"

Triangles:
Cut 1– 4" strip
Sub-cut 4 – 4" x 4"

From 4 assorted blue prints:
Cut 1– 3" strip of each fabric
Rectangle 3:
Sub-cut 1– 3" x 10" of each fabric (total of 4)
Rectangle 1:
Sub-cut 1– 3" x 8" of each fabric (total of 4)

From red, pink, green, gold prints
Rectangle 2:
Cut 1– 3" strip of each color.
Sub-cut 1– 3" x 8" of each color (total of 4)

From other red, pink, green, gold prints:
Rectangle 4:
Cut 1– 3" strip of each color.
Sub-cut 1– 3" x 10" of each color (total of 4)

Borders 5 & 6:
Cut 1– 13" strip
Sub-cut 4 each 5" x 13"
Sub-cut 4 each 5" x 10"

From 3 other assorted blue prints:
Cut 1– 3" strip of each fabric
Sashing 7:
Sub-cut 1– 3" x 13" from two blue prints (total of 2)
Sashing 8:
Sub-cut 1– 3" x 25" from the third blue print

Binding
Cut 3– 2½" strips

Batting Cutting Instructions

Label your cut pieces.

Center squares:
Cut 4– 6"x 6"

Rectangle 1:
Cut 4– 1" x 6"

Rectangle 2:
Cut 4– 1" x 6"

Rectangle 3:
Cut 4– 1" x 8"

Rectangle 4:
Cut 4– 1" x 8"

Border 5:
Cut 4– 3" x 8"

Border 6:
Cut 4– 3" x 11"

Sashing 7:
Cut 2– 1" x 11"

Sashing 8:
Cut 1– 1" x 23"

*Betty's Advice:
When cutting the batting, cut the longest pieces of batting first.*

37"

1" x 23"		1" x 8"	
X X X X X X X X X X X X X X X X X X X X X X X X			6" x 6"
3" x 11"	3" x 8"	X	
		X	1" x 6"
		X	X
		X	X
		X	6" x 6"
		X	X
		X	X
		X	X
1" x 11"	1" x 8"	X	X
		X	6" x 6"	X	6" x 6"
X X X X X X X X X		X		X	

18"

Cutting Diagram for Cotton Theory Batting (18" x 37")   *X denotes batting that is not used.*

Quilting Instructions

Insert quilting needle into your sewing machine. For best results, use a walking foot or even-feed foot when quilting.

Stitch suggestion: A zigzag 0.5 mm wide and 3.0 mm long will give the appearance of hand quilting, looking a little wobbly.

Thread suggestion: Match thread to the fabric for each side.

Center Squares:

1. Layer fabric and batting. With back fabric right-side down, place batting in center and place front fabric right side up.

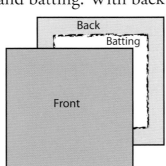

2. Press layers together with steam.

3. Place Adhesive Quilting Guide 4" to the right of sewing machine needle to guide fabric and provide straight quilting.

4. Quilt down the middle of each square.

5. Channel-stitch another row one presser-foot width away from the previous quilting.

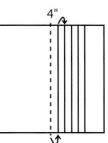

6. Repeat rows of channel stitching to within 1⅜" from edge of fabric, alternating directions to compensate for fabric shifting.

Note: Because the widths of presser feet vary, the number of quilting rows will vary.

7. Channel-stitch the other half of each square in the same manner.

8. Rotate each square one half turn.

9. Repeat steps 3 through 7 to create a grid of quilting.

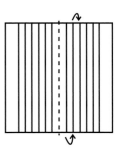

Front-Side Triangles:

Stitch suggestion: Use a 3.5 mm length straight stitch.

1. Mark a diagonal line on wrong sides of 4" squares.

2. With right sides together, place 4" squares on top of quilted center squares so that outside edges line up and diagonal lines extend across corners of center squares.

Top Left   Top Right

Bottom Left   Bottom Right

3. Stitch on the diagonal lines, through all layers.

4. Trim 4" squares ¼" from the diagonal lines, as shown in diagrams above. (Do not cut quilted center squares.)

5. Press triangles toward corners, so that right side of fabric is seen.

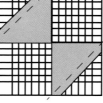

Betty's Advice: Label your quilted pieces so you can assemble your project easily.

Back-Side Triangles:

1. Mark a diagonal line on wrong sides of 4" squares.

2. With right sides together, place 4" squares on top of back-side center squares in different corners from front side.

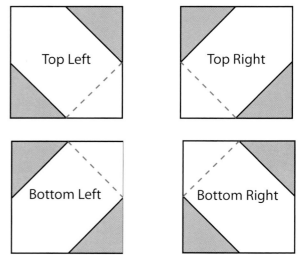

Top Left   Top Right

Bottom Left   Bottom Right

Red dotted lines indicate placement of 4" squares for back side.

3. Stitch on the diagonal lines, through all layers.

4. Trim the 4" squares ¼" from the diagonal lines. (Do not cut quilted center squares.)

5. Press triangles toward corner, so that right side of fabric is seen.

Rectangles 1 through 4 and Sashings 7 & 8:

1. Pair up front sides with back sides.

2. Layer fabric and batting. With back fabric right-side down, place one layer of batting in center, and place front fabric right side up.

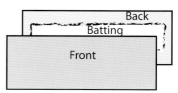

42

3. Press layers together with steam.

4. Place Adhesive Quilting Guide 1⅜" to the right of sewing machine needle.

5. Quilt down each side of the rectangles and sashings (total of two rows per rectangle or sashing).

Borders 5 & 6:

Stitch suggestion: Use a triple stitch (reinforcing stitch) 4.0 mm long.

Thread suggestion: Beige 50-weight cotton on top and in bobbin.

1. Pair up front-side and back-side borders.

2. Layer fabric and batting. With back fabric right-side down, place one layer of batting in center, and place front fabric right side up.

3. Press layers together with steam.

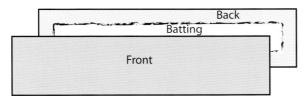

4. Place Adhesive Quilting Guide 2½" to the right of sewing machine needle.

5. Quilt down the middle of border pieces.

6. Place Adhesive Quilting Guide 1⅜" to the right of sewing machine needle.

7. Quilt down each side of border pieces.

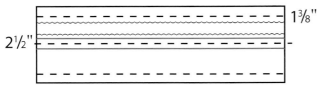

Red dotted lines indicate change of thread from beige to red in Step 8.

Note: For a narrow channel between rows of stitching, move the sewing machine's needle position to the right.

8. Change upper thread to red.

9. Using right side of presser foot as a guide, quilt a row one presser-foot width away on both sides of the middle quilting.

10. Change upper thread to blue.

11. Using a decorative stitch of your choice, stitch one or two rows inside wide channel on both halves of border pieces. (See diagram at bottom of previous column.)

Assembly Instructions

Insert topstitch needle into your sewing machine. Seam allowances will be finished on the front side using Highway and One-Way Street procedures.

Note: Use a 1" seam allowance when sewing your quilted pieces together.

Thread suggestion: Red 50-weight cotton on top and brown 50-weight cotton in bobbin.

1. With back sides together, use a 3.5 mm length straight stitch to sew Rectangle 1 to right-hand side of top-left center square and to sew Rectangle 2 (green back-side fabric) to left-hand side of top-left center square. Sew through all fabric layers.

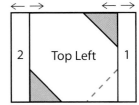

2. With back sides together, sew second Rectangle 1 to left-hand side of top-right center square and sew Rectangle 2 (red back-side fabric) to right-hand side of top-right center square.

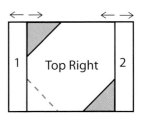

3. With back sides together, sew third Rectangle 1 to right-hand side of bottom-left center square and sew Rectangle 2 (pink back-side fabric) to left-hand side of bottom-left center square.

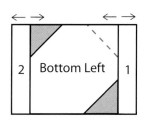

4. With back sides together, sew fourth Rectangle 1 to left-hand side of bottom-right center square and sew Rectangle 2 (gold back-side fabric) to right-hand side of bottom-right center square.

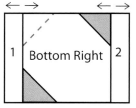

5. Press seams open on front side; then press the back side.

6. Finish seams using the Highway procedure. (See Techniques, Page 21.)

7. With back sides together, sew Rectangle 3 to the bottom of top-left center square and sew Rectangle 4 (green back-side fabric) to the top of top-left center square.

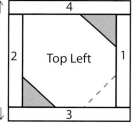

8. With back sides together, sew second Rectangle 3 to bottom of top-right center square and sew Rectangle 4 (red back-side fabric) to top of top-right center square.

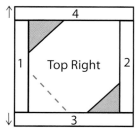

9. With back sides together, sew third Rectangle 3 to top of bottom-left center square and sew Rectangle 4 (pink back-side fabric) to bottom of bottom-left center square.

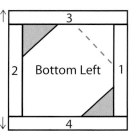

10. With back sides together, sew fourth Rectangle 3 to top of bottom-right center square and sew Rectangle 4 (gold back-side fabric) to bottom of bottom-right center square.

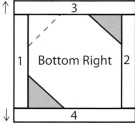

11. Press the back side; then press all seam allowances on front side toward the outside edges.

12. Finish seams using the One-Way Street procedure. (See Techniques, Page 22.)

Applying Borders 5 & 6:

1. With back sides together, sew Border 5 to side of the center units.

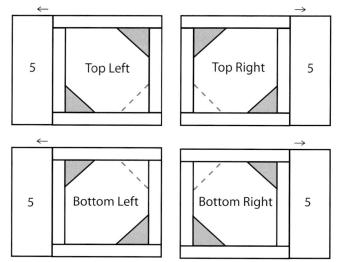

2. Press the back side; then press seam allowances on front side toward the outside edges.

3. Finish seams using the One-Way Street procedure.

4. With back sides together, sew Border 6 to top and bottom of center units.

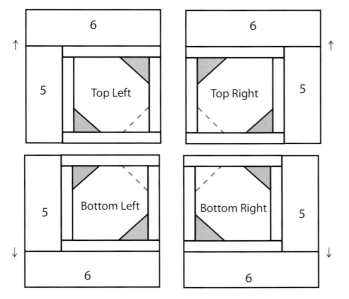

5. Press the back side; then press seam allowances on front side toward the outside edges.

6. Finish seams using the One-Way Street procedure.

Applying Sashings 7 & 8:

1. With back sides together, sew Sashing 7 to right-hand side of top-left unit and bottom-left unit.

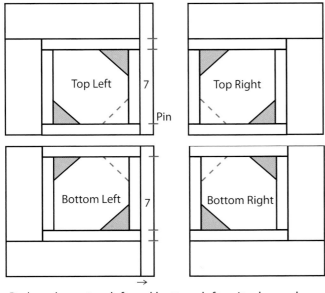

Red marks on top-left and bottom-left units show where intersections should align. (See Techniques, Page 23.)

2. Press the back side; then press seam allowances on front side toward the sashing.

3. Finish seams using the One-Way Street procedure.

4. Align intersections of the two top units and two bottom units of your project. (See Techniques, Page 23.)

5. With back sides together, sew top-left unit to top-right unit and sew bottom-left unit to bottom-right unit.

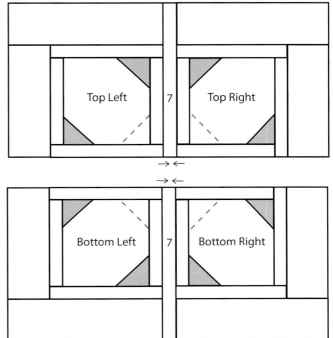

6. Press the back side; then press seam allowances on front side toward the sashing.

7. Finish seams using the One-Way Street procedure.

8. With back sides together, sew Sashing 8 to bottom of the top unit.

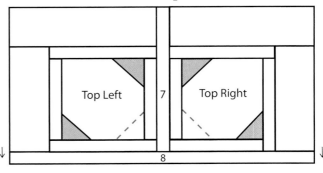

9. Press the back side; then press seam allowance on front side toward the sashing.

10. Finish seam using the One-Way Street procedure.

11. Align top-unit and bottom-unit intersections; then sew top unit to bottom unit.

12. Finish seam using the One-Way Street procedure.

Applying Binding:

1. Trim ⅝" from raw edges of project, leaving a ⅜" seam allowance on all sides.

2. Apply binding. (For instructions, see Binding section at end of this book.)

Finished Table Topper Diagram

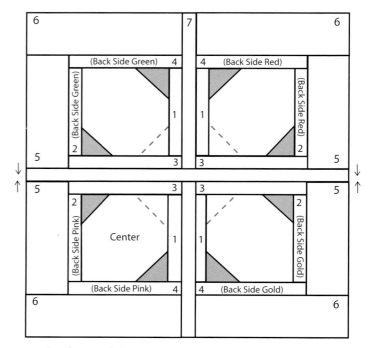

The front of this table topper has a prearranged placement of colors and fabrics, while the back has a scrappy appearance that is more informal. (See photos at beginning of this chapter.) Red lines on the diagram indicate the placement of triangles on the back side of the table topper.

Embroidered Table Topper
(23" x 23")

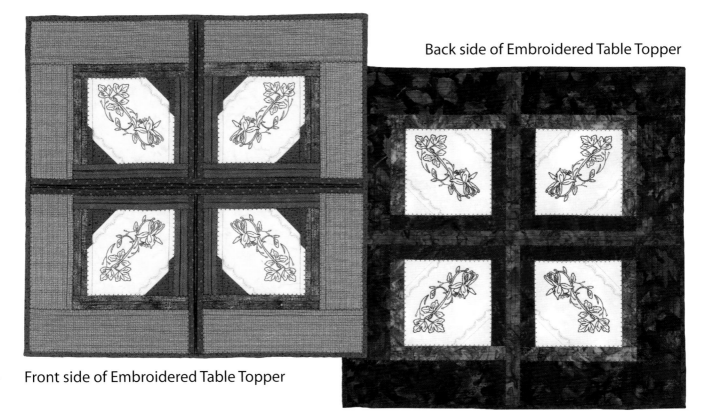

Back side of Embroidered Table Topper

Front side of Embroidered Table Topper

Yardage Requirements

(Based on 42-inch wide fabric)

Front Side

Center square:	¼ yd. pale yellow
Triangles:	⅛ yd. small barn red print
Rectangles 1 & 3:	⅜ yd. small green print
Rectangles 2 & 4:	⅜ yd. green/gray batik
Borders 5 & 6:	½ yd. barn red micro check
Sashings 7 & 8:	¼ yd. different small green print
Reversible binding:	¼ yd. small barn red print

Back Side

Center square:	¼ yd. pale gray
Rectangles 1 & 3:	⅜ yd. dark red batik
Rectangles 2 & 4:	⅜ yd. periwinkle blue batik
Borders 5 & 6:	½ yd. plum/purple print batik
Sashings 7 & 8:	¼ yd. plum batik
Reversible binding:	⅛ yd. purple batik

Batting

Cotton Theory Batting, 18" x 37"

Fabric Cutting Instructions

Cut carefully to ensure you have an adequate amount of fabric. Label your cut pieces for each side of the project. Cut strips on the crosswise grain of 42-inch wide fabric. (See Fabric Diagram 2 on Page 15.)

Front Side

Center square:
Cut 1– 8" strip
Sub-cut 4– 8" x 8"
(Sub-cuts are second cuts from the previous cut strip. See Fabric Diagram 3, Page 15.)

Triangles:
Cut 1– 4" strip
Sub-cut 8– 4" x 4"

From small green print:
Cut 1– 10" strip
> **Rectangle 3:**
> Sub-cut 4–
> 3" x 10"
>
> **Rectangle 1:**
> Sub-cut 4–
> 3" x 8"

From green/gray batik:
Cut 1– 10" strip
> **Rectangle 4:**
> Sub-cut 4–
> 3" x 10"
>
> **Rectangle 2:**
> Sub-cut 4–
> 3" x 8"

Borders:
Cut 1– 13" strip
> **Border 6:**
> Sub-cut 4–
> 5" x 13"
>
> **Border 5:**
> Sub-cut 4–
> 5" x 10"

Sashings:
Cut 2– 3" strips
> **Sashing 7:**
> Sub-cut 2–
> 3" x 13"
>
> **Sashing 8:**
> Sub-cut 1–
> 3" x 25"

Reversible binding:
Cut 3– 2¼" strips

Back Side

Center square:
Cut 1– 8" strip
Sub-cut 4– 8" x 8"

From dark red batik:
Cut 1– 10" strip
> **Rectangle 3:**
> Sub-cut 4–
> 3" x 10"
>
> **Rectangle 1:**
> Sub-cut 4–
> 3" x 8"

From periwinkle blue batik:
Cut 1– 10" strip
> **Rectangle 4:**
> Sub-cut 4–
> 3" x 10"
>
> **Rectangle 2:**
> Sub-cut 4–
> 3" x 8"

Borders:
Cut 1– 13" strip
> **Border 6:**
> Sub-cut 4–
> 5" x 13"
>
> **Border 5:**
> Sub-cut 4–
> 5" x 10"

Sashings:
Cut 2– 3" strips
> **Sashing 7:**
> Sub-cut 2–
> 3" x 13"
>
> **Sashing 8:**
> Sub-cut 1–
> 3" x 25"

Reversible binding:
Cut 3– 1¼" strips

Batting Cutting Instructions

Label your cut pieces.

Center squares:
Cut 4– 6"x 6"

Rectangle 1:
Cut 4– 1" x 6"

Rectangle 2:
Cut 4– 1" x 6"

Rectangle 3:
Cut 4– 1" x 8"

Rectangle 4:
Cut 4– 1" x 8"

Border 5:
Cut 4– 3" x 8"

Border 6:
Cut 4– 3" x 11"

Sashing 7:
Cut 2– 1" x 11"

Sashing 8:
Cut 1– 1" x 23"

Betty's Advice: When cutting the batting, cut the longest pieces of batting first.

37"

Cutting Diagram (Cotton Theory Batting):

- 1" x 23" | 1" x 8"
- X X X X X X X X X X X X X X X X X X X X X X X X X X X
- 3" x 11" | 3" x 8" | X (column) | 6" x 6"
- 1" x 6" | X (column)
- 6" x 6"
- 1" x 11" | 1" x 8" | 6" x 6" | 6" x 6"
- X X X X X X X X X
- **18"**

Cutting Diagram for Cotton Theory Batting (18" x 37")   *X denotes batting that is not used.*

Quilted Embroidery Instructions

Insert embroidery needle into your sewing machine. Test-stitch a sample; increase upper tension, if neccessary. Use embroidery design of your choice or follow the design suggestion in this section.

Thread suggestion: Dark green 40-weight cotton on top and dark red wool monét in bobbin.

Design: Cotton Theory Columbine. (See Page 152 for details on ordering.)

Center squares:

1. Layer fabric and batting. With back fabric right-side down, place batting in center and front fabric right side up.

2. Press layers together with steam.

3. Put a layer of water-soluble stabilizer in machine embroidery hoop.

4. Place layered fabric and batting on top of hooped stabilizer.

5. Machine baste into place.

6. Embroider design in center square, stitching through all layers.

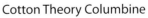

Cotton Theory Columbine

7. Repeat steps 1 through 6 for second center square.

8. Mirror-image the embroidery design; then repeat steps 1 through 6 to embroider the two remaining center squares.

Mirror image of
Cotton Theory Columbine

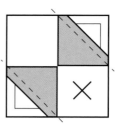 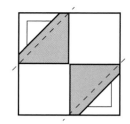

Top Left   **Top Right**

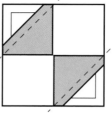 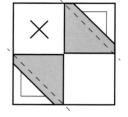

Bottom Left   **Bottom Right**

*X denotes center squares with
mirror-image embroidery*

9. Remove basting.

10. Dissolve stabilizer with water.

11. When center squares are thoroughly dry, press both sides.

Quilting Instructions

Insert quilting needle into your sewing machine. For best results, use a walking foot or even-feed foot when quilting.

Thread suggestion: Match thread to the fabric for each side.

Front-Side Triangles:

Stitch suggestion: Use a 3.5 mm length straight stitch.

1. Mark a diagonal line on wrong sides of 4" squares.

2. With right sides together, place 4" squares on top of embroidered center squares so that outside edges line up and diagonal lines extend across corners of center squares. Diagonal lines should run parallel to embroidered design.

3. Stitch on the diagonal lines, through all layers.

4. Trim the 4" squares and front-side fabric (top two layers) ¼" from diagonal lines, as indicated in diagrams in next column. (Do not cut batting or back-side fabric.)

5. Press triangles toward corners, so that right side of fabric is seen.

Note: Adding a decorative stitch near the seam of each triangle will fill in some of the unquilted space.

6. Select the decorative stitch of your choice. Then place edge of presser foot along seam line of each triangle and sew one row of decorative stitching. (Start and stop within 1" of raw edges.)

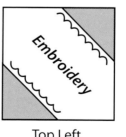 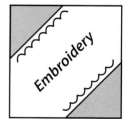

Top Left   **Top Right**

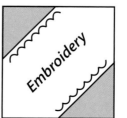 

Bottom Left   **Bottom Right**

Rectangles 1 through 4 and Sashings 7 & 8:

1. Pair up front-side and back-side pieces.

2. Layer fabric and batting. With back fabric right-side down, place one layer of batting in center, and place front fabric right side up.

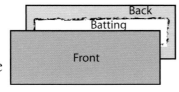

3. Press layers together with steam.

4. Place Adhesive Quilting Guide 1⅜" to the right of sewing machine needle.

5. Quilt down each side of the rectangles and sashings (total of two rows per rectangle or sashing).

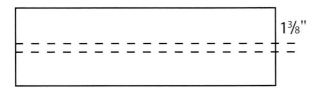

Borders 5 & 6:

1. Pair up front-side and back-side borders.

2. Layer fabric and batting. With back fabric right-side down, place one layer of batting in center, and place front fabric right side up.

3. Press layers together with steam.

4. Place Adhesive Quilting Guide 2½" to the right of sewing machine needle.

5. Quilt down the middle of the border pieces.

6. Channel-stitch one presser-foot width away from the previous quilting.

7. Channel-stitch two more rows, alternating directions while sewing to compensate for fabric shifting.

8. Channel-stitch the other half of each border in the same manner (total of seven rows).

Assembly Instructions

Insert topstitch needle into your sewing machine. Seam allowances will be finished on the front side of the project using Highway and One-Way Street procedures.

Note: Use a 1" seam allowance when sewing your quilted pieces together.

Thread suggestion: Barn red 50-weight cotton on top and dark blue 50-weight cotton in bobbin.

1. With back sides together, use a 3.5 mm length straight stitch to sew Rectangle 1 to right-hand side of top-left center square and to sew Rectangle 2 to left-hand side of top-left center square. Sew through all fabric layers.

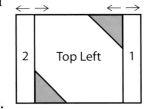

2. With back sides together, sew second Rectangle 1 to left-hand side of top-right center square and sew second Rectangle 2 to right-hand side of top-right center square.

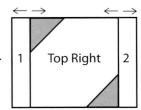

3. With back sides together, sew third Rectangle 1 to right-hand side of bottom-left center square and sew third Rectangle 2 to left-hand side of bottom-left center square.

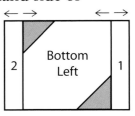

4. With back sides together, sew fourth Rectangle 1 to left-hand side of bottom-right center square and sew fourth Rectangle 2 to right-hand side of bottom-right center square.

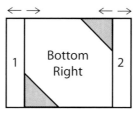

5. Press seams open on front side; then press the back side.

6. Finish seams using the Highway procedure. (See Techniques, Page 21.)

7. With back sides together, sew Rectangle 3 to bottom of top-left center square and sew Rectangle 4 to top of top-left center square.

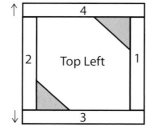

8. With back sides together, sew second Rectangle 3 to bottom of top-right center square and sew second Rectangle 4 to top of top-right center square.

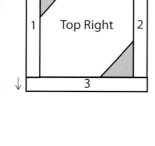

9. With back sides together, sew third Rectangle 3 to top of bottom-left center square and sew third Rectangle 4 to bottom of bottom-left center square.

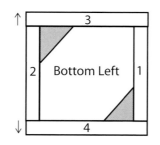

10. With back sides together, sew fourth Rectangle 3 to top of bottom-right center square and sew fourth Rectangle 4 to bottom of bottom-right center square.

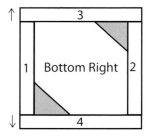

11. Press the back sides of center squares; then press all seam allowances on front sides toward outside edges.

12. Finish seams using the One-Way Street procedure. (See Techniques, Page 22.)

Applying Borders 5 & 6:

1. With back sides together, sew Border 5 to side of the center units.

2. Press the back side; then press seam allowances on front side toward outside edges.

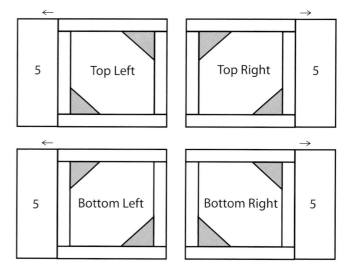

3. Finish seams using the One-Way Street procedure.

4. With back sides together, sew Border 6 to top and bottom of center units.

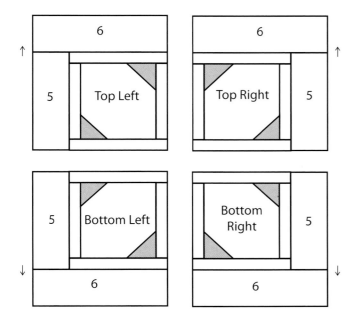

5. Press the back side; then press seam allowances on front side toward outside edges.

6. Finish seams using the One-Way Street procedure.

Applying Sashing 7 & 8:

1. With back sides together, sew Sashing 7 to right-hand side of top-left unit and bottom-left unit.

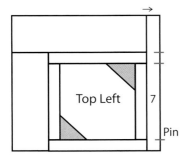
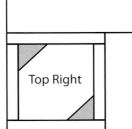
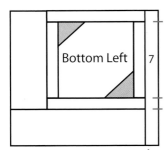
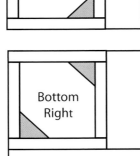

Red marks on top-left and bottom-left units show where intersections should align during assembly. (See Techniques, Page 23.)

2. Press the back side; then press seam allowances on front side toward the sashing.

3. Finish seams using the One-Way Street procedure.

4. Align intersections of the two top units and two bottom units of your project. (See Techniques, Page 23.)

5. With back sides together, sew top-left unit to top-right unit and sew bottom-left unit to bottom-right unit.

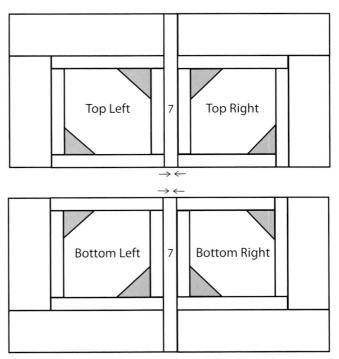

6. Press the back side; then press seam allowances on front side toward the sashing.

7. Finish seams using the One-Way Street procedure.

8. With back sides together, sew Sashing 8 to bottom of the top unit. (See diagram on next page.)

9. Press the back side; then press seam allowance on front side toward the sashing.

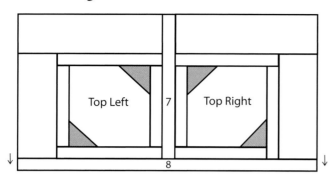

10. Finish seam using the One-Way Street procedure.

11. Align top-unit and bottom-unit intersections, and then sew top unit to bottom unit.

12. Finish seam using the One-Way Street procedure.

Finished Embroidered Table Topper Diagram

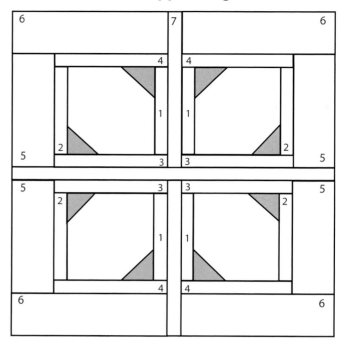

Applying Binding:

1. Trim ½" from raw edges of project, leaving a ½" seam allowance on all sides.

2. Apply reversible binding. (For instructions, see Binding section at end of this book.)

Cardinal Table Runner

(12"x 34")

Front side of Cardinal Table Runner

Yardage Requirements

(Based on 42-inch wide fabric)

This table runner lends itself to a scrappy appearance, with a mixture of prints and colors.

Front Side

Centers:	¼ yd. novelty print
Triangles:	⅛ yd. medium green
Rectangle 1:	⅛ yd. medium brown
Rectangle 2:	⅛ yd. dark green plaid
Rectangle 3:	⅛ yd. dark red
Rectangle 4:	⅛ yd. dark red
Rectangle 5:	⅛ yd. dark green print
Border:	¼ yd. beige print
	¼ yd. dark green

Back Side

Centers:	¼ yd. small floral print
Triangles:	⅛ yd. dark red
Rectangle 1:	⅛ yd. dark red check
Rectangle 2:	⅛ yd. beige/green print
Rectangle 3:	⅛ yd. dark green
Rectangle 4:	⅛ yd. dark green
Rectangle 5:	⅛ yd. medium green
Border:	¼ yd. beige print

Binding

¼ yd. dark green

Batting

Cotton Theory Batting, 18" x 34"

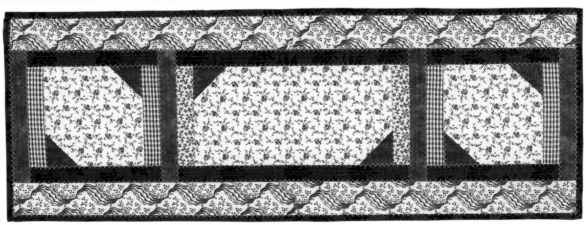

Back side of Cardinal Table Runner

Fabric Cutting Instructions

Cut carefully to ensure you have an adequate amount of fabric. Label your cut pieces for each side of the project. Cut strips on the crosswise grain of 42-inch wide fabric. (See Fabric Diagram 2 on Page 15.)

Front Side

Centers:
Cut 1– 8" strip
Sub-cut 2– 8" x 8"
Sub-cut 1– 8" x 14"
(Sub-cuts are second cuts from the previous cut strip. See Fabric Diagram 3, Page 15.)

Triangles:
Cut 1– 4" strip
Sub-cut 6– 4" x 4"

Rectangle 1:
Cut 1– 3" strip
Sub-cut 4– 3" x 8"

Rectangle 2:
Cut 1– 3" strip
Sub-cut 2– 3" x 8"

Rectangle 3:
Cut 1– 3" strip
Sub-cut 4– 3" x 10"

Rectangle 4:
Cut 1– 3" strip
Sub-cut 2– 3" x 16"

Rectangle 5:
Cut 1– 3" strip
Sub-cut 4– 3" x 10"

Border:
  Beige print:
  Cut 2– 4" strips
  Sub-cut 2– 4" x 23"
  Dark green:
  Cut 1– 4" strip
  Sub-cut 2– 4" x 18"

Back Side

Centers:
Cut 1– 8" strip
Sub-cut 2– 8" x 8"
Sub-cut 1– 8" x 14"

Triangles:
Cut 1– 4" strip
Sub-cut 6– 4" x 4"

Rectangle 1:
Cut 1– 3" strip
Sub-cut 4– 3" x 8"

Rectangle 2:
Cut 1– 3" strip
Sub-cut 2– 3" x 8"

Rectangle 3:
Cut 1– 3" strip
Sub-cut 4– 3" x 10"

Rectangle 4:
Cut 1– 3" strip
Sub-cut 2– 3" x 16"

Rectangle 5:
Cut 1– 3" strip
Sub-cut 4– 3" x 10"

Border:
Cut 2– 4" strips
Sub-cut 2– 4" x 36"

Binding
Cut 3– 2½" strips

Batting Cutting Instructions

Label your cut pieces.

Betty's Advice: When cutting the batting, cut the longest pieces of batting first.

34"

18"

| 2" x 34" |
| 2" x 34" |

6" x 6"

6" x 12"   6" x 6"

6" x 6"

1" x 8"
1" x 8"
1" x 8"
1" x 8"
1" x 8"
1" x 8"
1" x 8"
1" x 8"

1" x 6"
1" x 6"
1" x 6"
1" x 6"
1" x 6"

1" x 14"
1" x 14"

Cutting Diagram for Cotton Theory Batting (18" x 34")

Centers:
Cut 2– 6" x 6"
Cut 1– 6" x 12"

Rectangle 1:
Cut 4– 1" x 6"

Rectangle 2:
Cut 2– 1" x 6"

Rectangle 3:
Cut 4– 1" x 8"

Rectangle 4:
Cut 2– 1" x 14"

Rectangle 5:
Cut 4– 1" x 8"

Border:
Cut 2– 2" x 34"

Quilting Instructions

Insert quilting needle into your sewing machine. For best results, use a walking foot or even-feed foot when quilting.

Stitch suggestion: Lengthen straight stitch to 3.5 mm.

Thread suggestion: Match thread to the fabric for each side.

Center Rectangle:

1. Layer fabric and batting. With back fabric right-side down, place 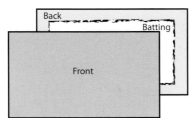 batting in center, and place front fabric right side up.

2. Press layers together with steam.

3. On front-side fabric, mark a vertical line 7" from one of the short sides of rectangle. This is the middle of the rectangle.

4. Quilt down the middle.

5. Channel-stitch another row one presser-foot width away from the previous quilting.

6. Repeat rows of channel stitching to within 1⅜" from raw edge of fabric, alternating directions to compensate for fabric shifting.

Note: Because presser-foot widths vary, the number of quilting rows will vary.

7. Channel-stitch the other half of the rectangle in the same manner.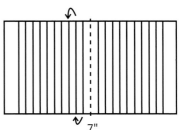

Center Squares:

1. Layer fabric and batting. With back fabric right-side down, place batting in center, and place front fabric right side up.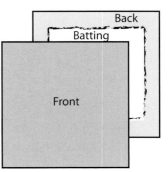

2. Press layers together with steam.

3. Place Adhesive Quilting Guide 4" to the right of sewing machine needle.

4. Quilt down the middle.

5. Channel-stitch another row one presser-foot width away from the previous quilting.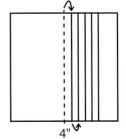

6. Repeat rows of channel stitching to within 1⅜" from raw edge of fabric, alternating directions.

7. Channel-stitch the other half of the rectangle in the same manner.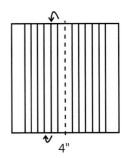

Front-Side Triangles:

1. Mark a diagonal line on wrong side of the 4" squares.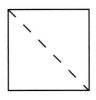

2. With right sides together, place 4" squares on top of front-side center squares and rectangle so that outside edges line up and diagonal lines extend across corners.

3. Stitch on the diagonal lines, through all layers.

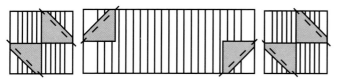

4. Trim each 4" square ¼" from the diagonal line, as shown in diagram. (Do not cut quilted center square or rectangle.)

5. Press triangles toward corners, so that right side of fabric is seen.

Back-Side Triangles:

1. Mark a diagonal line on wrong sides of 4" squares.

2. With right sides together, place 4" squares on top of back-side center squares and rectangle in opposite corners from front side.

Red dotted lines indicate placement of 4" squares for back side.

3. Stitch on the diagonal lines, through all layers.

4. Trim each 4" square ¼" from the diagonal lines. (Do not cut quilted center squares and rectangle.)

5. Press triangles toward corners, so that right side of fabric is seen.

Rectangles 1 through 5:

1. Pair up front-side and back-side rectangles.

2. Layer fabric and batting. With back fabric right-side down, place one layer of batting in center, and place front fabric right side up.

3. Press layers together with steam.

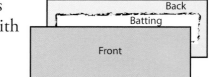

4. Place Adhesive Quilting Guide 1⅜" to the right of sewing machine needle.

5. Quilt down each side of the rectangles (total of two rows per rectangle).

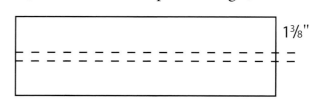

1⅜"

Borders:

1. With right sides together, place one dark green and one beige front-side border piece perpendicular to each other, with ends overlapping, as shown in diagram.

2. Join pieces with a mitered seam (sewn at a 45-degree angle).

3. Repeat steps 1 and 2 for other dark green and beige front-side border pieces.

4. Trim seams to ¼".

5. Press seams open and press borders flat.

6. Measure front-side borders, and trim to 4" x 36".

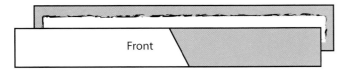

7. Pair up front-side and back-side borders.

8. Layer fabric and batting. With back fabric right-side down, place one layer of batting in center, and place front fabric right side up.

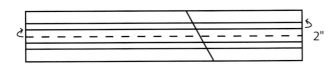

9. Press layers together with steam.

10. Place Adhesive Quilting Guide 2" to the right of sewing machine needle.

11. Quilt down the middle of border.

12. Channel-stitch another row one presser-foot width away from the previous quilting (about ⅜").

13. Reverse directions, and channel-stitch an additional row one presser-foot width away from the previous quilting.

14. Channel-stitch the other half of the border in the same manner (total of five rows).

Assembly Instructions

Insert topstitch needle into your sewing machine. Seam allowances will be finished on the front side of the project using Highway and One-Way Street procedures.

Note: Use a 1" seam allowance when sewing your quilted pieces together.

Thread suggestion: Medium tan 50-weight cotton on top and in bobbin.

1. With back sides together, use a 3.5 mm length straight stitch to sew Rectangle 1 to the sides of the center squares and to sew Rectangle 2 to the sides of the center rectangle. Sew through all fabric layers.

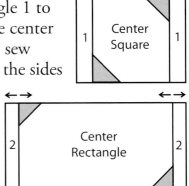

2. Press seams open on front side; then press the back side.

3. Finish seams using the Highway procedure. (See Techniques, Page 21.)

4. With back sides together, sew Rectangle 3 to the top and bottom of the center squares and sew Rectangle 4 to the top and bottom of the center rectangle.

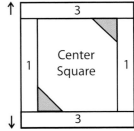

5. Press the back side. Then press all seam allowances on front side toward the outside edges.

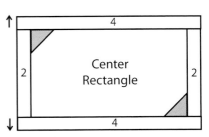

6. Finish seams using the One-Way Street procedure. (See Techniques, Page 22.)

7. With back sides together, sew Rectangle 5 to the sides of the center squares.

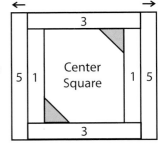

8. Press the back side; then press all seam allowances on front side toward outside edges.

9. Finish seams using the One-Way Street procedure.

Connecting Centers:

1. Align intersections of the center squares and center rectangle. (See Techniques, Page 23.)

2. With back sides together, sew center squares to short sides of center rectangle.

3. Press the back side; then press seam allowances on front side toward Rectangle 5.

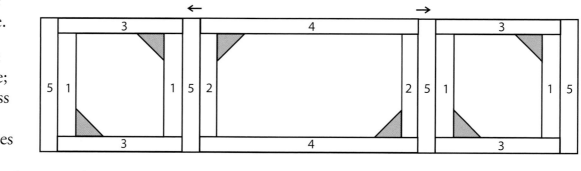

4. Finish seams using the One-Way Street procedure.

Applying Borders:

1. With back sides together, sew borders to top and bottom of center unit.

2. Press the back side; then press seam allowance on front side toward the borders.

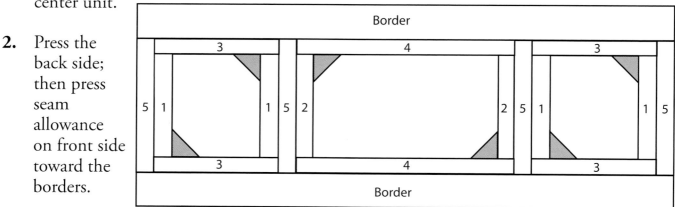

3. Finish seam using the One-Way Street procedure.

Applying Binding:

1. Trim ⅝" from raw edges of project, leaving a ⅜" seam allowance on all sides.

2. Apply binding. (For instructions, see Binding section at end of this book.)

Add an attractive accent to your home with a Cotton Theory quilting project such as this Cardinal Table Runner.

Two Seasons Table Runner
Embroidered (12"x 34")

Front side of Two Seasons Table Runner

Yardage Requirements

(Based on 42-inch wide fabric)

This table runner lends itself to a scrappy appearance, with a mixture of prints and colors.

Front Side

Centers:	¼ yd. beige
Triangles:	⅛ yd. medium green
Rectangle 1:	⅛ yd. red plaid
Rectangle 2:	⅛ yd. green print
Rectangle 3:	⅛ yd. medium green
Rectangle 4:	⅛ yd. red stripe
Rectangle 5:	⅛ yd. dark green print
Border:	¼ yd. light print

Back Side

Centers:	¼ yd. gold print
Triangles:	⅛ yd. medium red
Rectangle 1:	⅛ yd. orange print
Rectangle 2:	⅛ yd. rust print
Rectangle 3:	⅛ yd. light brown print
Rectangle 4:	⅛ yd. dark green
Rectangle 5:	⅛ yd. gold plaid
Border:	¼ yd. dark print

Binding

¼ yd. dark green

Batting

Cotton Theory Batting, 18" x 34"

Back side of Two Seasons Table Runner

Fabric Cutting Instructions

Cut carefully to ensure you have an adequate amount of fabric. Label your cut pieces for each side of the project. Cut strips on the crosswise grain of 42-inch wide fabric. (See Fabric Diagram 2 on Page 15.)

Front Side

Centers:
Cut 1– 8" strip
Sub-cut 2– 8" x 8"
Sub-cut 1– 8" x 14"
(Sub-cuts are second cuts from the previous cut strip. See Fabric Diagram 3 on Page 15.)

Triangles:
Cut 1– 4" strip
Sub-cut 6– 4" x 4"

Rectangle 1:
Cut 1– 3" strip
Sub-cut 4– 3" x 8"

Rectangle 2:
Cut 1– 3" strip
Sub-cut 2– 3" x 8"

Rectangle 3:
Cut 1– 3" strip
Sub-cut 4– 3" x 10"

Rectangle 4:
Cut 1– 3" strip
Sub-cut 2– 3" x 16"

Rectangle 5:
Cut 1– 3" strip
Sub-cut 4– 3" x 10"

Border:
Cut 2– 4" strips
Sub-cut 2– 4" x 36"

Back Side

Centers:
Cut 1– 8" strip
Sub-cut 2– 8" x 8"
Sub-cut 1– 8" x 14"

Triangles:
Cut 1– 4" strip
Sub-cut 6– 4" x 4"

Rectangle 1:
Cut 1– 3" strip
Sub-cut 4– 3" x 8"

Rectangle 2:
Cut 1– 3" strip
Sub-cut 2– 3" x 8"

Rectangle 3:
Cut 1– 3" strip
Sub-cut 4– 3" x 10"

Rectangle 4:
Cut 1– 3" strip
Sub-cut 2– 3" x 16"

Rectangle 5:
Cut 1– 3" strip
Sub-cut 4– 3" x 10"

Border:
Cut 2– 4" strips
Sub-cut 2– 4" x 36"

Binding
Cut 3– 2½" strips

Batting Cutting Instructions

Label your cut pieces.

Betty's Advice:
When cutting the batting, cut the longest pieces of batting first.

Cutting Diagram for Cotton Theory Batting (18" x 34")

Centers:
Cut 2– 6"x 6"
Cut 1– 6" x 12"

Rectangle 1:
Cut 4– 1" x 6"

Rectangle 2:
Cut 2– 1" x 6"

Rectangle 3:
Cut 4– 1" x 8"

Rectangle 4:
Cut 2– 1" x 14"

Rectangle 5:
Cut 4– 1" x 8"

Border:
Cut 2– 2" x 34"

Quilted Embroidery Instructions

Insert embroidery needle into your sewing machine. Test-stitch a sample; increase upper tension, if neccessary. Use embroidery design of your choice, or follow design suggestion in this section. (For more quilted embroidery advice, see Techniques, Page 24.)

Thread suggestion: Dark olive and medium brown 50-weight cotton on top and hunter green and dark brown 50-weight cotton in bobbin.

Design: Cactus Punch (Sig 45) Pine Bough Sprig in center squares; Pfaff 347/Design 10 (steps 2 and 3 only) in center rectangle. Designs available through sewing machine dealers.

Center Squares and Rectangle:

1. Layer fabric and batting. With back fabric right-side down, place batting in center, and place front fabric right side up.

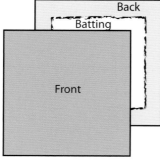

2. Press layers together with steam.

3. Insert a layer of water-soluble stabilizer in machine embroidery hoop.

4. Place layered fabric and batting on top of hooped stabilizer.

5. Machine baste into place.

6. Embroider designs in center rectangle and in one center square, stitching through all layers.

Cactus Punch (Sig 45) Pine Bough Sprig

Pfaff 347/Design 10 (steps 2 and 3 only)

7. For second center square, mirror-image the embroidery design, and repeat steps 1 through 6 to embroider.

Mirror image of Pine Bough Sprig

8. Remove basting in squares and rectangle.

9. Dissolve stabilizer with water.

10. Press both sides of embroidered centers when they're thoroughly dry.

Quilting Instructions

Insert quilting needle into your sewing machine. For best results, use a walking foot or even-feed foot when quilting.

Stitch suggestion: Lengthen straight stitch to 3.5 mm.

Thread suggestion: Match thread to the fabric for each side.

Front-Side Triangles:

1. Mark a diagonal line on wrong side of 4" squares.

2. With right sides together, place 4" squares on top of front-side center squares and rectangle so that outside edges line up and diagonal lines extend across corners.

Note: The embroidery in the squares is a directional design. Make sure the embroidered squares are mirror images of each other when you place the 4" squares on them.

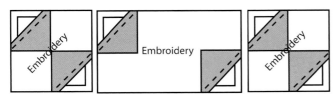

3. Stitch on the diagonal lines, through all layers.

4. Trim the 4" squares and the front-side fabric (top two layers) ¼" from the diagonal lines, as shown in the diagram. (Do not cut batting or back-side fabric.)

5. Press triangles toward corners, so that right side of fabric is seen.

Back-Side Triangles:

1. Mark a diagonal line on wrong sides of 4" squares.

2. With right sides together, place 4" squares on top of back-side center squares and rectangle in opposite corners from front side.

3. Stitch on the diagonal lines, through all layers.

Red dotted lines indicate placement of 4" squares and diagonal lines on back side

4. Trim the 4" squares and the back-side fabric (top two layers) ¼" from the diagonal lines. (Do not cut batting or front-side fabric.)

5. Press triangles toward corners, so that right side of fabric is seen.

Center Squares:

1. Place edge of presser foot along seam of triangles and quilt one row of stitching to create a box around embroidery.

Center Rectangle:

1. Place edge of presser foot along seam of a triangle and begin quilting. Follow triangle seam and as you approach edge of rectangle, pivot 1⅜" from the raw edges. Continue to spiral around and quilt three to four rows. End the spiral by backstitching with a small (0.5 mm) stitch length.

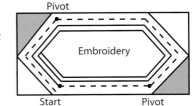

Rectangles 1 through 5:

1. Pair up front-side and back-side rectangles.

2. Layer fabric and batting. With back fabric right-side down, place one layer of batting in center, and place front fabric right side up.

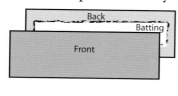

3. Press layers together with steam.

4. Place Adhesive Quilting Guide 1⅜" to the right of sewing machine needle.

5. Quilt down each side of the rectangles (total of two rows per rectangle).

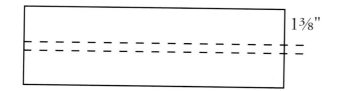

1⅜"

Borders:

1. Layer fabric and batting. With back fabric right-side down, place one layer of batting in center, and place front fabric right side up.

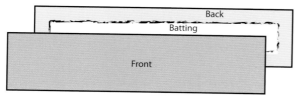

2. Press layers together with steam.

3. Place Adhesive Quilting Guide 2" to the right of sewing machine needle.

4. Quilt down the middle of border.

5. Channel-stitch another row one presser-foot width away from the previous quilting (about ⅜").

6. Reverse directions, and channel-stitch an additional row one presser-foot width away from the previous quilting.

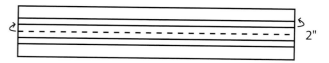

2"

7. Channel-stitch the other half of the border in the same manner. You should have a total of five rows of channel-stitching.

Assembly Instructions

Insert topstitch needle into your sewing machine. Seam allowances will be finished on the front side of the project using Highway and One-Way Street procedures.

Note: Use a 1" seam allowance when sewing your quilted pieces together.

Thread suggestion: Medium tan 50-weight cotton on top and in bobbin.

1. With back sides together, use a 3.5 mm length straight stitch to sew Rectangle 1 to the sides of the center squares and to sew Rectangle 2 to the sides of the center rectangle. Sew through all fabric layers.

	Center Square	
1		1

	Center Rectangle	
2		2

2. Press seams open on front side; then press the back side.

3. Finish seams using the Highway procedure. (See Techniques, Page 21.)

4. With back sides together, sew Rectangle 3 to the top and bottom of the center squares and sew Rectangle 4 to top and bottom

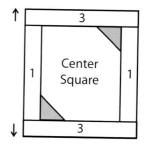

of the center rectangle.

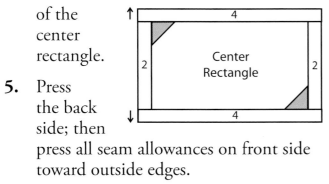

5. Press the back side; then press all seam allowances on front side toward outside edges.

6. Finish seams using the One-Way Street procedure. (See Techniques, Pages 22.)

7. With back sides together, sew Rectangle 5 to the sides of the center squares.

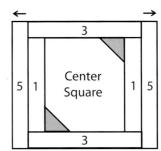

8. Press the back side; then press all seam allowances on front side toward the outside edges.

9. Finish seams using the One-Way Street procedure.

Connecting Centers:

1. Align intersections of the center squares and center rectangle. (See Techniques, Page 23.)

2. With back sides together, sew center squares to short sides of center rectangle.

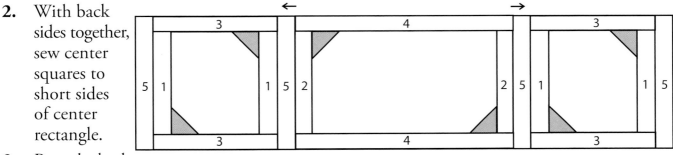

3. Press the back side; then press seam allowances on front side toward Rectangle 5.

4. Finish seams using the One-Way Street procedure.

Applying Borders:

1. With back sides together, sew borders to top and bottom of center unit.

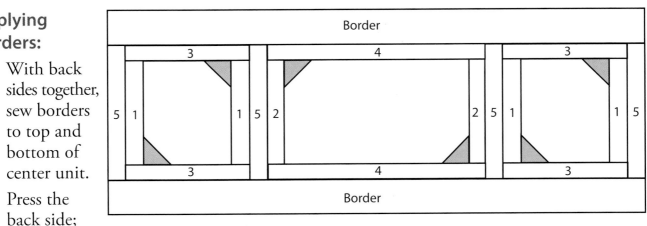

2. Press the back side; then press seam allowance on front side toward the borders.

3. Finish seam using the One-Way Street procedure.

Applying Binding:

1. Trim ⅝" from raw edges of project, leaving a ⅜" seam allowance on all sides.

2. Apply binding. (For instructions, see Binding section at end of this book.)

Outside of tote: Variegated yarn was used in the sewing machine bobbin to create this embroidered bobbin work on the Two-Image Tote.

Outside of tote (back view): The quilted embroidery on this image was done with green/tan variegated cotton thread.

Inside of reversible tote: Red/purple variegated thread makes this quilted embroidery stand out. Using thread in the upper part of the sewing machine and yarn in the bobbin (as shown above) allows you to create two different types of embroidery at once.

Inside of reversible tote (back view): Narrow silk ribbon (2mm) was wound on the bobbin to produce this image. Variegated thread (as shown above) was used in the upper part of the sewing machine. The embroidery designs on this page are from Cactus Punch Quilting Vol. 4.

Two-Image Tote
(10" x 14" x 4")

Yardage Requirements

(Based on 42-inch wide fabric)

This tote bag is meant to have a scrappy appearance, with a mixture of prints and colors.

Front Side (Outside)

Center rectangles:	¼ yd. each of 2 assorted light colors
Triangles:	⅛ yd. each of 2 assorted dark colors
Rectangle 1:	3" x 8" each of 4 assorted medium prints
Rectangle 2:	⅛ yd. each of 2 assorted medium prints
Rectangle 3:	3" x 10" each of 4 assorted dark prints
Rectangle 4:	⅛ yd. each of 2 assorted dark prints
Rectangle 5:	¼ yd. each of 2 assorted dark prints
Reversible binding:	⅛ yd. medium color

Back Side (Inside)

Center rectangles:	¼ yd. each of 2 assorted light colors
Triangle:	⅛ yd. each of 2 assorted medium colors
Rectangle 1:	3" x 8" each of 4 assorted light prints
Rectangle 2:	⅛ yd. each of 2 assorted medium prints
Rectangle 3:	3" x 10" each of 4 assorted light prints
Rectangle 4:	⅛ yd. each of 2 assorted dark prints
Rectangle 5:	¼ yd. each of 2 assorted dark prints
Reversible binding:	⅛ yd. medium color
Handles	¼ yd. tan
Batting	Cotton Theory Batting, 18" x 32"
Other Supplies	10– 1" assorted buttons

Fabric Cutting Instructions

Cut carefully to ensure you have an adequate amount of fabric. Label your cut pieces for each side of the project. Cut strips on the crosswise grain of 42-inch wide fabric. (See Fabric Diagram 2 on Page 15.)

Betty's Advice:
Cut front-side and back-side fabrics together. This eliminates pairing them up later .

Front Side
Outside of tote

Center rectangles:
From each of 2 assorted light colors:
Cut 1– 8" strip
Sub-cut 1– 8" x 14"
(Sub-cuts are second cuts from a previous cut strip. See Fabric Diagram 3. Page 15.)

Triangles:
From each of 2 assorted dark colors:
Cut 1– 4" strip
Sub-cut 4– 4" x 4"

Rectangle 1:
From each of 4 assorted medium prints:
Cut 1– 3" x 8"

More on next page

Rectangle 2:
From each of 2 assorted medium prints:
Cut 1– 3" strip.
Sub-cut 2– 3" x 16"

Rectangle 3:
From each of 4 assorted dark prints:
Cut 1– 3" x 10"

Rectangle 4:
From each of 2 assorted dark prints:
Cut 1– 3" strip
Sub-cut 1– 3" x 34"

Rectangle 5:
From each of 2 assorted dark prints:
Cut 1– 4" strip
Sub-cut 1– 4" x 34"

Reversible binding:
Cut 1– 2¼" strip

Back Side
Inside of tote

Center rectangles:
From each of 2 assorted light colors:
Cut 1– 8" strip
Sub-cut 1– 8" x 14"

Triangles:
From each of 2 assorted medium colors:
Cut 1– 4" strip
Sub-cut 4– 4" x 4"

Rectangle 1:
From each of 4 assorted light prints:
Cut 1– 3" x 8"

Rectangle 2:
From each of 2 assorted medium prints:
Cut 1– 3" strip
Sub-cut 2– 3" x 16"

Rectangle 3:
From each of 4 assorted light prints:
Cut 1– 3" x 10"

Rectangle 4:
From each of 2 assorted dark prints:
Cut 1– 3" strip
Sub-cut 1– 3" x 34"

Rectangle 5:
From each of 2 assorted dark prints:
Cut 1– 4" strip
Sub-cut 1– 4" x 34"

Reversible binding:
Cut 1– 1¼" strip

Handles
Cut 2– 3" strips
Sub-cut 4– 3" x 18"

Batting Cutting Instructions

Label your cut pieces. Cut longest pieces first.

Center rectangles:
Cut 2– 6"x 12"

Rectangle 1:
Cut 4– 1" x 6"

Rectangle 2:
Cut 4– 1" x 14"

Rectangle 3:
Cut 4– 1" x 8"

Rectangle 4:
Cut 2– 1" x 32"

Rectangle 5:
Cut 2– 2" x 32"

Handles:
Cut 4– 1" x 17½"

32"

| 2" x 32" |
| 1" x 32" |

6" x 12" | 6" x 12"

1" x 14"

1" x 8"   1" x 6"

1" x 17½"

X (batting not used)

18"

Cutting Diagram for Cotton Theory Batting (18" x 32")

X denotes batting that is not used

Quilted Embroidery and Bobbin Work Instructions

Insert embroidery needle into your sewing machine. Test-stitch a sample; adjust bobbin tension and upper tension, if neccessary. Use embroidery design of your choice, or follow design suggestions in this section. (For more quilted embroidery and bobbin work advice, see Techniques, Pages 24–25.)

Designs for center rectangles: Cactus Punch Quilting Vol. 4, Hand Sewing and Porridge designs, enlarged to fit in a 6" x12" stitch field. Designs available through local sewing machine dealers.

Thread suggestions for center rectangles: For Hand Sewing design, red/purple variegated 40-weight cotton on top and variegated dark purples 39 g yarn in bobbin. For Porridge design, green/tan variegated 40-weight cotton on top and variegated harvest colors 2 mm silk ribbon in bobbin.

Note: By embroidering center rectangles upside down (back-side fabric up), you can feature bobbin work on the front of your project.

Center Rectangles:

1. Layer fabric and batting. With back fabric right-side down, place batting in center, and place front fabric right side up.

2. Press layers together with steam.

3. Place one layered center rectangle in machine embroidery hoop upside down, with back fabric facing right side up.

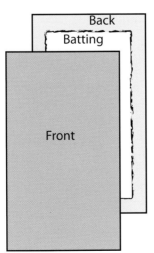

4. Embroider first design.

Hand Sewing
(from Cactus Punch Quilting Vol. 4)

5. Change thread in upper sewing machine and bobbin, and switch to second embroidery design.

6. Place second layered center rectangle in machine embroidery hoop with front fabric facing right side up.

Note: This will give you bobbin work on one outside center panel of the finished tote and quilted embroidery on the other outside center panel. If you want bobbin work on both outside center panels, embroider both with back fabric facing right side up.

7. Embroider second design.

Porridge
(from Cactus Punch Quilting Vol. 4)

Quilting Instructions

Insert quilting needle into your sewing machine. For best results, use a walking foot or even-feed foot when quilting

Stitch: Use a 3.5 mm length straight stitch.

Thread suggestion: Match thread to the fabric for each side.

Triangles:

You will be sewing front-side and back-side triangles at the same time.

1. Mark a diagonal line on wrong sides of front-side 4" squares.

2. With right sides together, place 4" squares on fronts and backs of center rectangles so that outside edges line up and diagonal lines extend across corners of center rectangles.

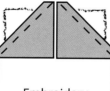

3. Stitch on the diagonal lines, through all layers.

4. Trim the 4" squares and the front-side and back-side fabrics ¼" from the diagonal lines, as shown in illustration. (Do not cut batting.)

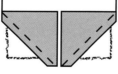

5. Press front-side and back-side triangles toward corners, so that right side of fabric is seen.

6. With a decorative scallop stitch, quilt along seams of triangles on front side of center rectangles, starting 1" from raw edge on each end (at dots shown in illustration).

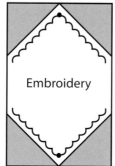

Rectangles 1 through 4:

1. Pair up front-side and back-side rectangles.

2. Layer fabric and batting. With back fabric right-side down, place one layer of batting in center, and place front fabric right side up.

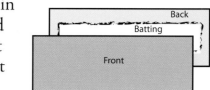

3. Press layers together with steam.

4. Place Adhesive Quilting Guide 1⅜" to the right of sewing machine needle.

5. Quilt down each side of the rectangles (total of two rows per rectangle).

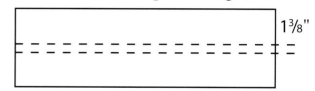

Rectangle 5:

1. Pair up front-side and back-side rectangles.

2. Layer fabric and batting. With back fabric right-side down, place one layer of batting in center, and place front fabric right side up.

3. Press layers together with steam.

4. Place Adhesive Quilting Guide 1⅜" to the right of sewing machine needle.

5. Quilt down each side of the rectangles.

6. Channel-stitch another row toward the middle, one presser-foot width away from the previous quilting (total of four rows).

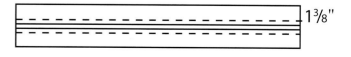

Assembly Instructions

Insert topstitch needle into your sewing machine. Seam allowances will be finished on the front side of the project using Highway and One-Way Street procedures.

Note: Use a 1" seam allowance when sewing your quilted pieces together.

1. With back sides together, sew Rectangle 1 to the top and bottom (short sides) of each center rectangle. Sew through all fabric layers.

2. Press seams open on front side; then press the back side.

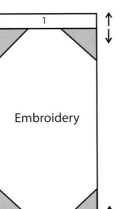

3. Finish seams using the Highway procedure. (See Techniques, Page 21.)

4. With back sides together, sew Rectangle 2 to long sides of each center rectangle.

5. Press the back side; then press all seam allowances on front side toward the outside edges.

6. Finish seams using the One-Way Street procedure. (See Techniques, Page 22.)

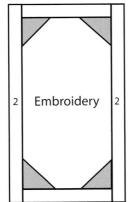

7. With back sides together, sew one Rectangle 3 to a second Rectangle 3.

8. Press seams open on front side; then press the back side.

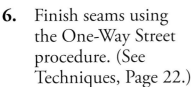

9. Finish seams using the Highway procedure.

10. Repeat steps 7 through 9 with the third and fourth Rectangle 3.

11. With back sides together, sew the two Rectangle 3 units together.

12. Press seams open on front side; then press the back side.

13. Finish seams using the Highway procedure.

Combining Center Rectangles:

Bobbin work will be facing up on one center rectangle and facing down on second center rectangle.

1. With back sides together, sew the Rectangle 3 unit to the bottom of one center rectangle.

2. Press the back side; then press seam allowances on front side toward the Rectangle 3 unit.

3. Finish seam using the One-Way Street procedure.

4. With back sides together, sew Rectangle 3 unit to bottom of remaining center rectangle.

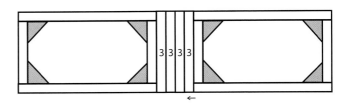

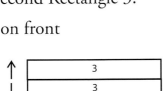

5. Press the back side; then press seam allowances on front side toward the Rectangle 3 unit.

6. Finish seam using the One-Way Street procedure.

7. With back sides together, sew Rectangle 4 to Rectangle 5.

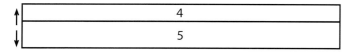

8. Press seam open on front side; then press the back side.

9. Finish seam using the Highway procedure.

10. Repeat steps 7 through 9 for remaining Rectangles 4 and 5.

11. With back sides together, sew Rectangle 4 units to sides of center unit.

12. Press the back side; then press seam allowances on front side toward Rectangle 4 units.

13. Finish seams using the One-Way Street procedure.

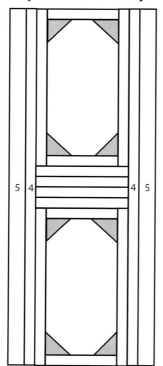

14. With back sides together, fold center unit in half.

15. Sew the sides with a ⅜" seam; backstitch at beginning and end.

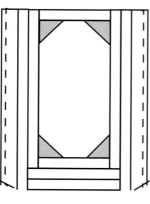

16. Clip corners.

17. Press side seams open.

18. Turn back side out.

Note: You will be constructing a French seam, which will conceal raw edges of previous ⅜" seam.

19. Press tote flat.

20. Sew a ⅝" seam down each side.

21. Press each side seam in one direction.

22. Machine baste top edges.

23. Turn front side out.

Note: You will be forming a mock box pleat with a mitered corner (45-degree angle).

24. Separate and flatten front and back at the bottom corner of Rectangle 5 on one side of tote.

25. Center the seam and fold fabric at bottom toward the seam to form a pointed, mitered corner.

26. Pin in place.

27. Stitch across the folded corner, starting and stopping ½" from the ends; backstitch at beginning and end.

28. Fold triangle point up against side of tote; sew 1" button to the triangle and tote to hold the triangle in place.

29. Repeat steps 24 through 28 on other side of tote.

Applying Binding:

1. Trim ½" from raw edges at top of tote, leaving a ½" seam allowance on all sides.

2. Apply reversible binding. (For instructions, see Binding section at end of this book.)

Completing Handles:

1. Pair up two pieces of handle fabric with right sides together (no batting in middle).

2. Sew a ¼" seam on each end, creating a short, wide tube of fabric.

3. Press seams open.

4. Separate fabric layers and rotate seams so they are 4" from ends when tube is flat.

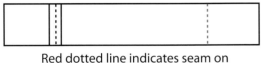

Red dotted line indicates seam on underside of fabric tube.

5. Place two layers of batting down the center on top layer of fabric tube. (Batting will reach to ends.)

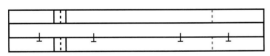

Note: The handles have a double layer of batting to create a thicker quilted piece.

6. Pin batting in place through top layer of fabric only.

7. Turn fabric tube right side out.

8. Press tube flat.

9. Place Adhesive Quilting Guide 1½" to the right of the sewing machine needle.

10. Quilt down the middle of the flattened tube, sewing through all layers and removing pins.

11. Repeat steps 1 through 10 for the other two pieces of handle fabric.

12. Fold raw edges of each handle ½" toward the middle, and press in place.

13. Fold long sides so they meet at the quilting line in the middle, and pin in place.

14. Using a decorative stitch of your choice, sew down the middle through both folded sides at the same time. (This is a Highway handle.)

15. With a triple stitch (reinforcing stitch), sew down each side of the handles, close to the outside edges; backstitch at beginning and end.

16. Position handles on tote and attach with heavy thread and 1" buttons. Place buttons on inside and outside of tote.

Dress up a dreary space with this Appliqued Wall Hanging
made with Cotton Theory quilting techniques.

Appliquéd Wall Hanging
(40"x 32")

Yardage Requirements

(Based on 42-inch wide fabric)

Front Side

Center rectangles:	½ yd. soft green
Appliqué pieces:	9" x 12" of 5 assorted synthetic suede colors – green, brown, tan, gold, sand
Background squares:	¼ yd. soft green print
Triangles:	¼ yd. black print
Rectangle 1:	¼ yd. red plaid
Rectangle 2:	¼ yd. dark red print
Rectangle 3:	⅜ yd. green print
Rectangle 4:	½ yd. green/ black stripe
Rectangle 5:	⅜ yd. red print
Rectangle 6:	⅛ yd. different red print
Rectangle 7:	¼ yd. light green print
Border:	⅝ yd. soft green

Back Side *(not shown)*

Center rectangles:	½ yd. soft blue
Background squares:	¼ yd. soft blue print
Triangles:	¼ yd. dark tan
Rectangle 1:	¼ yd. dark brown print
Rectangle 2:	¼ yd. medium brown print
Rectangle 3:	⅜ yd. med. blue plaid
Rectangle 4:	½ yd. med. blue print
Rectangle 5:	⅜ yd. brown/ black print
Rectangle 6:	⅛ yd. different brown/black print
Rectangle 7:	¼ yd. medium blue
Border:	⅝ yd. blue/tan micro check

Binding
⅜ yd. brown print

Batting
Cotton Theory Batting, 18" x 81"

Fabric Cutting Instructions

Cut carefully to ensure you have an adequate amount of fabric. Label your cut pieces for each side of the project. Cut strips on the crosswise grain of 42-inch wide fabric. (See Fabric Diagram 2 on Page 15.)

For Each Side

Center rectangles:
Cut 2– 8" strips
Sub-cut 4– 8" x 14"
(Sub-cuts are second cuts from the previous strips. See Fabric Diagram 3, Page 15.)

Background squares:
Cut 1– 8" strip
Sub-cut 4– 8" x 8"

Triangles:
Cut 2– 4" strips
Sub-cut 12– 4" x 4"

Rectangle 1:
Cut 1– 8" strip
Sub-cut 8– 3" x 8"

Rectangle 2:
Cut 1– 8" strip
Sub-cut 8– 3" x 8"

Rectangle 3:
Cut 1– 10" strip
Sub-cut 8– 3" x 10"

Rectangle 4:
Cut 1– 16" strip
Sub-cut 8– 3" x 16"

Rectangle 5:
Cut 1– 10" strip
Sub-cut 10– 3" x 10"

Rectangle 6:
Cut 1– 3" strip
Sub-cut 4– 3" x 10"

Rectangle 7:
Cut 2– 3" strips
Sub-cut 2– 3" x 36"

Borders:
Cut 4– 5" strips
Sub-cut 2– 5" x 36"
Sub-cut 2– 5" x 34"

More on next page

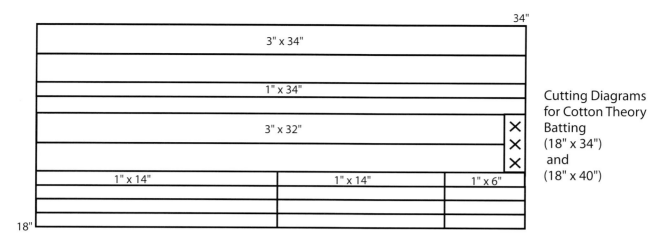

Cutting Diagrams
for Cotton Theory
Batting
(18" x 34")
 and
(18" x 40")

3" x 34"

1" x 34"

3" x 32"

1" x 14"   1" x 14"   1" x 6"

X denotes batting that is not used

40"

1" x 8"   1" x 8"

6" x 12"   6" x 12"

1" x 6"

6" x 6"   6" x 6"

18"

Binding
Cut 4– 2½" strips

Appliqué Pieces

*Pieces are shown
actual size on last
two pages of this
chapter. Trace or
copy appliqués and
use for cutting.*

Green synthetic suede:
Cut 4 No. 5 pieces (Page 87)
Cut 4 No. 5 pieces mirror-imaged (Page 88)

Brown synthetic suede:
Cut 2 No. 4 pieces (Page 87)
Cut 2 No. 4 pieces mirror-imaged (Page 88)

Tan synthetic suede:
Cut 2 No. 1 pieces (Page 87)
Cut 2 No. 1 pieces mirror-imaged (Page 88)

Gold synthetic suede:
Cut 2 No. 3 pieces (Page 87)
Cut 2 No. 3 pieces mirror-imaged (Page 88)

Sand synthetic suede:
Cut 2 No. 2 pieces (Page 87)
Cut 2 No. 2 pieces mirror-imaged (Page 88)

Batting Cutting Instructions

Label your cut pieces. Cut longest pieces of
batting first.

Center rectangles:
Cut 4– 6"x 12"

Squares:
Cut 4– 6" x 6"

Rectangle 1:
Cut 8– 1" x 6"

Rectangle 2:
Cut 8– 1" x 6"

Rectangle 3:
Cut 8– 1" x 8"

Rectangle 4:
Cut 8– 1" x 14"

Rectangle 5:
Cut 10– 1" x 8"

Rectangle 6:
Cut 4– 1" x 8"

Rectangle 7:
Cut 2– 1" x 34"

Borders:
Cut 2– 3" x 34"
Cut 2– 3" x 32"

A decorative, circular stitch adds a scribble effect to the edges of these appliquéd pieces.

Quilting & Appliqué Instructions

Insert quilting needle into your sewing machine. For best results, use a walking foot or even-feed foot when quilting. Please label your quilted pieces.

Center Rectangles:

Thread suggestion: Match thread to the fabric for front side, and use a contrast thread for back side.

Stitch suggestion: For appliqués, use a decorative stitch with a circular appearance for a scribble effect. Set the stitch length at 3.0 mm and the width at 3.0 mm.

1. Layer fabric and batting. With back fabric right-side down, place one layer of batting in center and place front fabric right side up.

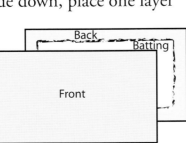

2. Press layers together with steam.

3. Place appliqué pieces on front side of center rectangles. Use spray adhesive or a glue stick to temporarily hold pieces in place.

Appliqués for Row 1 and
left side of Row 2

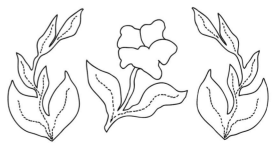

Appliqués for Row 3 and
right side of Row 2

79

4. Using a decorative scribble stitch, sew outside edges of appliqués, through all layers.

5. Stitch veins in appliqués with a 3.5 mm length straight stitch, backstitching at beginning and end.

Front-Side Background Squares:

1. Layer fabric and batting for background squares. With back fabric right-side down, place layer of batting in center and place front fabric right side up.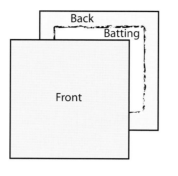

2. Press layers together with steam.

3. Mark a diagonal line on wrong side of all 4" squares.

4. With right sides together, place one front-side 4" square on top of each front-side background square so that outside edges line up and diagonal line extends across corner.

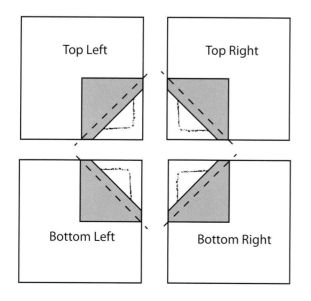

5. Stitch on the diagonal lines, through all layers.

6. Trim the 4" squares and front-side fabric (top 2 layers) ¼" from the diagonal lines, as shown in illustration in previous column. (Do not cut batting or back-side fabric.)

7. Press triangles toward corners, so that right side of fabric is seen.

8. Place edge of presser foot along seam of one triangle and stitch a diagonal row.

9. Channel-stitch another row one presser-foot width away from the previous quilting (about ⅜").

10. Repeat rows of channel stitching diagonally across the background square, alternating directions to compensate for fabric shifting.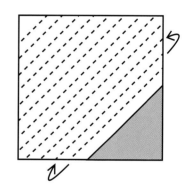

11. Complete steps 8 through 10 on remaining three background squares.

Back-Side Background Squares

1. With right sides together, place back-side 4" squares on top of back-side background squares in opposite corners from front side. (See diagram at top of next page.)

2. Stitch on the diagonal lines, through all layers.

3. Trim the 4" squares ¼" from the diagonal lines. (Do not cut quilted background squares.)

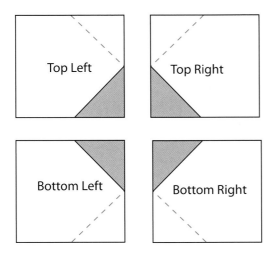

Red dotted lines indicate placement of 4" squares on back side after front-side triangles are completed.

4. Press triangles toward corners, so that right side of fabric is seen.

Front-Side Center Rectangles:

1. With right sides together, place front-side 4" squares on top of front-side center rectangles, in positions shown in diagrams, so that outside edges line up and diagonal lines extend across corners.

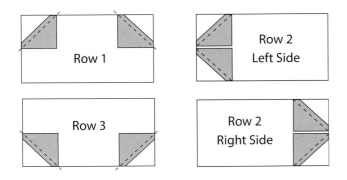

2. Stitch on the diagonal lines, through all layers.

3. Trim the 4" squares and front-side fabric (top 2 layers) ¼" from the diagonal lines, as shown in illustrations. (Do not cut batting or back-side fabric.)

4. Press triangles toward corners, so that right side of fabric is seen.

Back-Side Center Rectangles:

1. With right sides together, place back-side 4" squares on top of back-side center rectangles in opposite corners from front side.

2. Stitch on the diagonal lines, through all layers.

3. Trim the 4" squares and back-side fabric (top two layers) ¼" from the diagonal lines. (Do not cut batting or front-side fabric.)

4. Press triangles toward corners, so that right side of fabric is seen.

Red dotted lines indicate placement of 4" squares on back side

Rectangles 1 through 7:

1. Layer fabric and batting. With back fabric right-side down, place one layer of batting in center and place front fabric right side up.

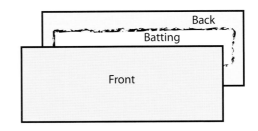

2. Press layers together with steam.

3. Place Adhesive Quilting Guide 1⅜" to the right of sewing machine needle.

4. Quilt down each side of the rectangles (total of two rows per rectangle)

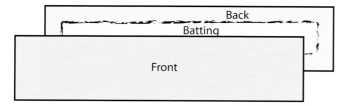

1⅜"

Borders:

Stitch suggestion: Use a triple stitch 4.0 mm long.

Thread suggestion: Black 40-weight cotton on top and brown 50-weight cotton in bobbin.

1. Layer fabric and batting. With back fabric right-side down, place layer of batting in center and place front fabric right side up.

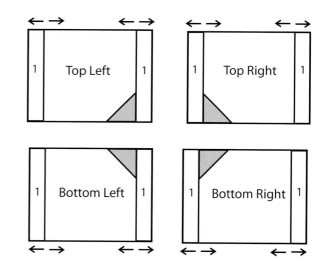

Back
Batting
Front

2. Press layers together with steam.

3. Place Adhesive Quilting Guide 2½" to the right of sewing machine needle.

4. Quilt down the middle of border.

5. Move needle position to right side to create a wider channel (about a ½" space).

6. Channel-stitch another row one presser-foot width away on both sides of the middle.

Thread change: Red 40-weight cotton on top and in bobbin.

2½"

7. Channel-stitch an additional row one presser-foot width away from the previous quilting on both sides of the middle (total of five rows).

Assembly Instructions

Insert topstitch needle into your sewing machine. Seam allowances will be finished on the front side of the project using Highway and One-Way Street procedures.

Note: Use a 1" seam allowance when sewing your quilted pieces together.

Thread suggestion: Green 40-weight cotton on top and brown 50-weight cotton in bobbin.

1. With back sides together, sew Rectangle 1 to the sides of the background squares. Sew through all fabric layers.

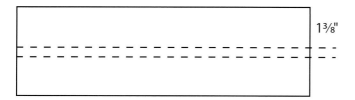

2. Press seams open on front side; then press the back side.

3. Finish seams using the Highway procedure. (See Techniques, Page 21.)

4. With back sides together, sew Rectangle 2 to sides of center rectangles.

5. Press seams open on front side; then press the back side.

6. Finish seams using the Highway procedure.

7. With back sides together, sew Rectangle 3 to the top and bottom of the background squares, as indicated in diagrams below.

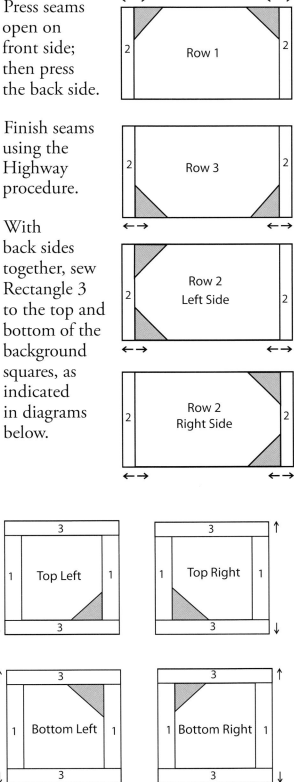

8. Press the back side; then press all seam allowances on front side toward outside edges.

9. Finish seams using the One-Way Street procedure. (See Techniques, Page 22.)

10. With back sides together, sew Rectangle 4 to the top and bottom of the center rectangles.

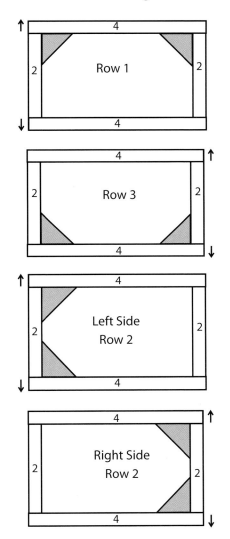

11. Press the back side; then press all seam allowances on front side toward outside edges.

12. Finish seams using the One-Way Street procedure.

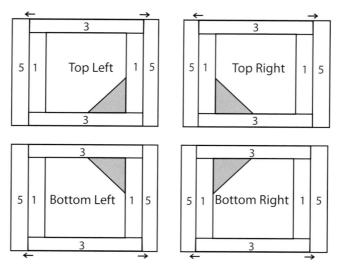

13. With back sides together, sew Rectangle 5 to the sides of the background squares.

14. Press the back side; then press all seam allowances on front side toward outside edges.

15. Finish seams using the One-Way Street procedure.

Connecting Background Squares and Center Rectangles

1. Align intersections of Row 1 and Row 3 background squares and center rectangles. (See Techniques, Page 23.)

2. With back sides together, sew background squares to short sides of center rectangles.

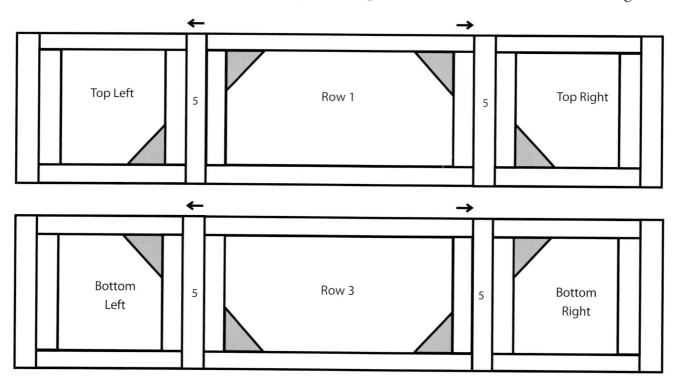

3. Press the back side; then press all seam allowances on front side toward Rectangle 5.

4. Finish seams using the One-Way Street procedure.

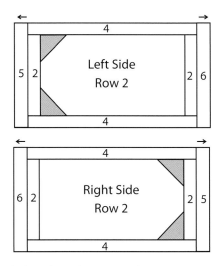

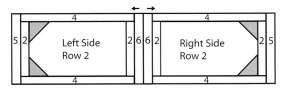

5. With back sides together, sew Rectangle 5 to the outside edge of the Row 2 center rectangles, and sew Rectangle 6 to the inside edge of the Row 2 center rectangles, as shown above.

6. Press the back side; then press all seam allowances on front side toward outside edges.

7. Finish seams using the One-Way Street procedure.

8. Align intersections of Row 2 center rectangles. (See Techniques, Page 23.)

9. With back sides together, sew Row 2 center rectangles together.

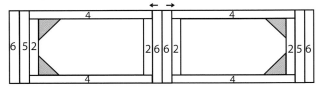

10. Press seams open on front side of project; then press the back side.

11. Finish seams using the Highway procedure.

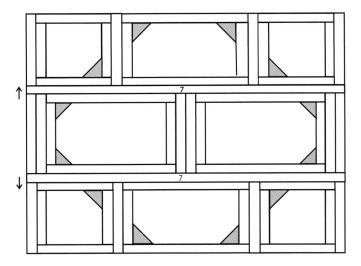

12. With back sides together, sew Rectangle 6 to outside edges of Row 2.

13. Press the back side; then press all seam allowances on front side toward outside edges.

14. Finish seams using the One-Way Street procedure.

15. With back sides together, sew Rectangle 7 to the top and bottom of Row 2.

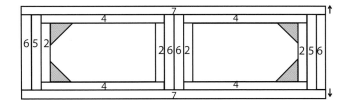

16. Press the back side; then press all seam allowances on front side toward outside edges.

17. Finish seams using the One-Way Street procedure.

Connecting the Rows:

1. With back sides together, sew Row 1 to Row 2.

2. Press seam allowances on front side toward Rectangle 7.

3. Finish seam using the One-Way Street procedure.

4. With back sides together, sew Row 2 to Row 3.

5. Repeat steps 2 and 3.

Applying Borders:

1. With back sides together, sew borders (5" x 36") to top and bottom of your wall hanging.

2. Press the back side; then press all seam allowances on front side toward the outside edges.

3. Finish seams using the One-Way Street procedure.

4. With back sides together, sew borders (5" x 34") to the sides of your wall hanging.

5. Press the back side; then press all seam allowances on front side toward the outside edges.

6. Finish seams using the One-Way Street procedure.

Applying Binding:

1. Trim ⅝" from raw edges of project, leaving a ⅜" seam allowance on all sides.

2. Apply binding (For instructions, see Binding section at end of this book.)

Hanging Your Quilt:

Because Cotton Theory projects are reversible, the best way to hang your decorative quilt is with a wall-mount quilt holder.

Finished Appliquéd Wall Hanging Diagram

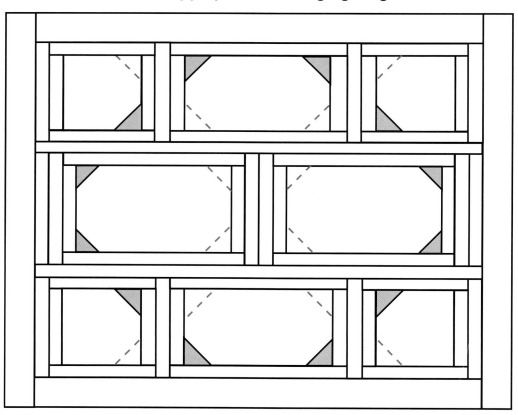

Red lines on the diagram indicate placement of triangles on the back side of the wall hanging.

Wall Hanging Appliqués
Actual Size

Appliqué designs by Betty Cotton

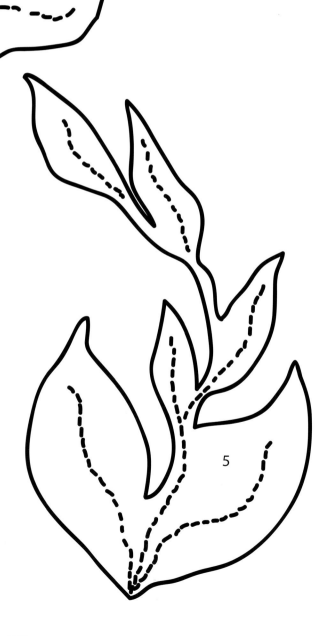

3

2

1

4

Wall Hanging Appliqués
Actual Size
(Mirror Image)

Appliqué designs by Betty Cotton

5

Cardinal Wall Hanging
(40" x 32")

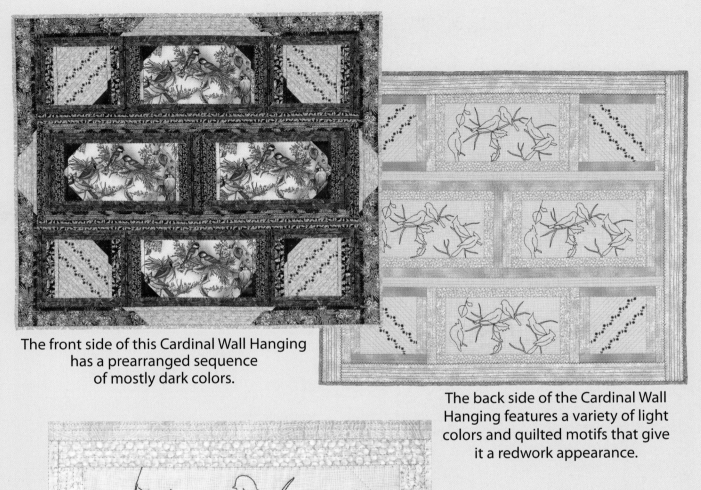

The front side of this Cardinal Wall Hanging has a prearranged sequence of mostly dark colors.

The back side of the Cardinal Wall Hanging features a variety of light colors and quilted motifs that give it a redwork appearance.

This close-up of the back side shows embroidery details.

Fabric can determine how a project will be quilted. By outlining the cardinals and a few branches on the front side and by using contrasting thread on the back side, this Cardinal Wall Hanging offers two completely different looks.

— *Cardinal Wall Hanging by Betty Cotton*

Tick-Tack-Toe Quilt
(Variable Sizes)

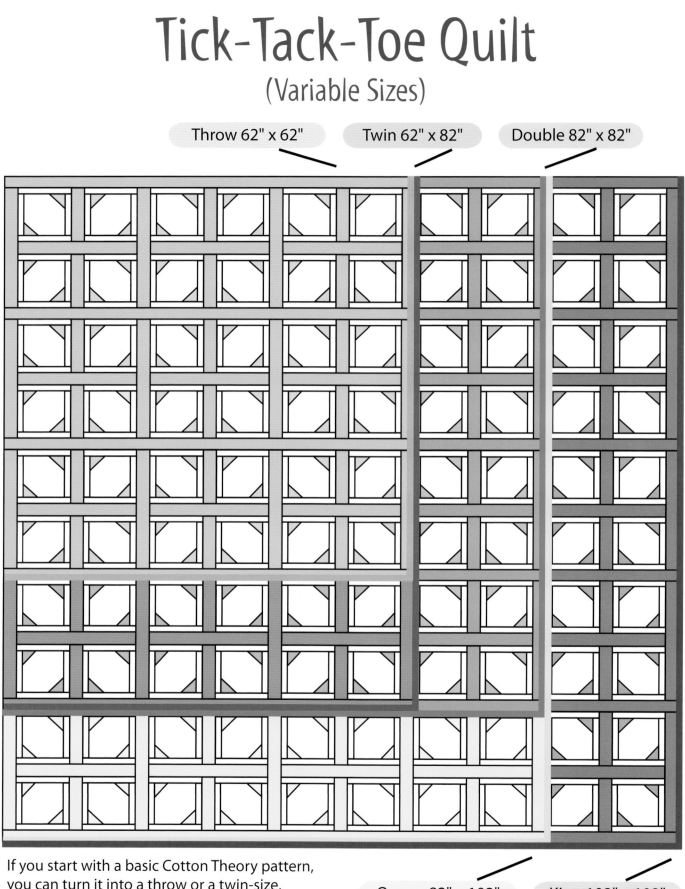

Throw 62" x 62"   Twin 62" x 82"   Double 82" x 82"

Queen 82" x 102"   King 102" x 102"

If you start with a basic Cotton Theory pattern, you can turn it into a throw or a twin-size, double-size, queen-size or king-size quilt. The instructions for Tick-Tack-Toe show you how.

Tick-Tack-Toe

Yardage Requirements

(Based on 42-inch wide fabric)

	Throw	Twin	Double	Queen	King
Front Side					
Center square:	1⅞ yd.	2⅜ yd.	3⅛ yd.	3¾ yd.	4⅝ yd.
Triangles:	1 yd.	1¼ yd.	1⅝ yd.	1⅞ yd.	2⅜ yd
Rectangle 1:	1½ yd.	1¾ yd.	2⅜ yd.	2⅞ yd.	3½ yd.
Rectangle 2:	1¾ yd.	2⅛ yd.	3 yd.	3½ yd.	4⅜ yd.
Rectangle 3:	⅝ yd.	1 yd.	1¼ yd.	1¼ yd.	1½ yd.
Rectangle 4:	⅝ yd.	1¼ yd.	1¼ yd.	1¼ yd.	1¾ yd.
Rectangle 5:	1¼ yd.	1¼ yd.	1¼ yd.	1¾ yd.	1¾ yd.
Rectangle 6:	1⅞ yd.	1⅞ yd.	2½ yd.	2½ yd.	3 yd.
Back Side					
Center square:	1⅞ yd.	2⅜ yd.	3⅛ yd.	3¾ yd.	4⅝ yd.
Rectangle 1:	1½ yd.	1¾ yd.	2⅜ yd.	2⅞ yd.	3½ yd.
Rectangle 2:	1¾ yd.	2⅛ yd.	3 yd.	3½ yd.	4⅜ yd.
Rectangle 3:	⅝ yd.	1 yd.	1¼ yd.	1¼ yd.	1½ yd.
Rectangle 4:	⅝ yd.	1¼ yd.	1¼ Toe.	1¼ yd.	1¾ yd.
Rectangle 5:	1¼ yd.	1¼ yd.	1¼ yd.	1¾ yd.	1¾ yd.
Rectangle 6:	1⅞ yd.	1⅞ yd.	2½ yd.	2½ yd.	3 yd.
Binding					
Yardage:	⅝ yd.	⅝ yd.	¾ yd.	⅞ yd.	⅞ yd.
Batting					
Cotton Theory Batting:	18" x 6¼ yd.	18" x 8 yd.	18" x 11 yd.	18" x 14 yd.	18" x 17 yd.

Tick-Tack-Toe Throw (9 blocks – 62" x 62")

Fabric Cutting Instructions

Cut carefully to ensure you have an adequate amount of fabric. Label your cut pieces for each side. Cut strips on the crosswise grain of 42-inch wide fabric. (See Fabric Diagram 2 on Page 15.)

For Each Side

Center square:
Cut 8– 8" strips
Sub-cut 36 – 8" x 8"
(Sub-cuts are second cuts from the original strips. See Fabric Diagram 3 on Page 15.)

Triangles (front side only):
Cut 8– 4" strips
Sub-cut 72– 4" x 4"

Rectangle 1:	Cut 6– 8" strips Sub-cut 72– 3" x 8"
Rectangle 2:	Cut 6– 10" strips Sub-cut 72– 3" x 10"
Rectangle 3:	Cut 2– 10" strips Sub-cut 18– 4" x 10"
Rectangle 4:	Cut 1– 20" strip Sub-cut 9– 4" x 20"
Rectangle 5:	Cut 2– 20" strips Sub-cut 12– 4" x 20"
Rectangle 6:	Cut 1– 64" strip Sub-cut 4– 4" x 64"
Binding	Cut 7– 2½" strips

Batting Cutting Instructions

Center squares:
Cut 36– 6"x 6"

Rectangle 1:
Cut 72– 1" x 6"

Rectangle 2:
Cut 72– 1" x 8"

Rectangle 3:
Cut 18– 2" x 8"

Rectangle 4:
Cut 9– 2" x 18"

Rectangle 5:
Cut 12– 2" x 18"

Rectangle 6:
Cut 4– 2" x 62"

See batting cutting diagrams on Page 93.

Betty's Advice: When cutting the batting, cut longest pieces of batting first, and label your cut pieces.

62"

2" x 62"

2" x 18"	2" x 18"	2" x 18"	X
			X
			X
			X

18"

72"

| 2" x 8" | 2" x 8" | 1" x 8" | 1" x 8" | 1" x 8" | 1" x 8" | 1" x 6" | 1" x 6" | 1" x 6" | 1" x 6" |

18"

54"

6" x 6"

2" x 18"

× × × × × × ×

18"

36"

6" x 6"

18"

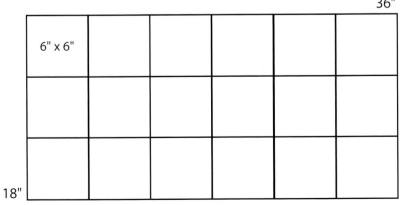

Cotton Theory Batting Cutting Diagrams for 62" x 62" Throw (Page 92)

X denotes batting that is not used.

93

Tick-Tack-Toe Twin (12 blocks – 62" x 82")

Fabric Cutting Instructions

Cut carefully to ensure you have an adequate amount of fabric. Label your cut pieces for each side. Cut strips on the crosswise grain of 42-inch wide fabric. (See Fabric Diagram 2 on Page 15.)

For Each Side

Center square:
Cut 10– 8" strips
Sub-cut 48 – 8" x 8"
(Sub-cuts are second cuts from the original strips. See Fabric Diagram 3 on Page 15.)

Triangles(front side only):
Cut 10– 4" strips
Sub-cut 96– 4" x 4"

Rectangle 1: Cut 7– 8" strips
Sub-cut 96– 3" x 8"

Rectangle 2: Cut 7– 10" strips
Sub-cut 96– 3" x 10"

Rectangle 3: Cut 3– 10" strips
Sub-cut 24– 4" x 10"

Rectangle 4: Cut 2– 20" strips
Sub-cut 12– 4" x 20"

Rectangle 5: Cut 2– 20" strips
Sub-cut 15– 4" x 20"

Rectangle 6: Cut 1– 64" strip
Sub-cut 5– 4" x 64"

Binding Cut 8– 2½" strips

Batting Cutting Instructions

Center squares:
Cut 48– 6"x 6"

Rectangle 1:
Cut 96– 1" x 6"

Rectangle 2:
Cut 96– 1" x 8"

Rectangle 3:
Cut 24– 2" x 8"

Rectangle 4:
Cut 12– 2" x 18"

Rectangle 5:
Cut 15– 2" x 18"

Rectangle 6:
Cut 5– 2" x 62"

Betty's Advice:
When cutting the batting, cut longest pieces of batting first, and label your cut pieces.

Tick-Tack-Toe Double (16 blocks – 82" x 82")

Fabric Cutting Instructions

Cut carefully to ensure you have an adequate amount of fabric. Label your cut pieces for each side. Cut strips on the crosswise grain of 42-inch wide fabric. (See Fabric Diagram 2 on Page 15.)

For Each Side

Center square:
Cut 13– 8" strips
Sub-cut 64 – 8" x 8"
(Sub-cuts are second cuts from the original strips. See Fabric Diagram 3 on Page 15.)

Triangles (front side only):
Cut 13– 4" strips
Sub-cut 128– 4" x 4"

Rectangle 1: Cut 10– 8" strips
Sub-cut 128– 3" x 8"

Rectangle 2: Cut 10– 10" strips
Sub-cut 128– 3" x 10"

Rectangle 3: Cut 4– 10" strips
Sub-cut 32– 4" x 10"

Rectangle 4: Cut 2– 20" strips
Sub-cut 16– 4" x 20"

Rectangle 5: Cut 2– 20" strips
Sub-cut 20– 4" x 20"

Rectangle 6: Cut 1– 84" strip
Sub-cut 5– 4" x 84"

Binding Cut 9– 2½" strips

Batting Cutting Instructions

Center squares:
Cut 64– 6"x 6"

Rectangle 1:
Cut 128– 1" x 6"

Rectangle 2:
Cut 128– 1" x 8"

Rectangle 3:
Cut 32– 2" x 8"

Rectangle 4:
Cut 16– 2" x 18"

Rectangle 5:
Cut 20– 2" x 18"

Rectangle 6:
Cut 5– 2" x 82"

Betty's Advice: When cutting the batting, cut longest pieces of batting first, and label your cut pieces.

Tick-Tack-Toe Queen (20 blocks – 82" x 102")

Fabric Cutting Instructions

Cut carefully to ensure you have an adequate amount of fabric. Label your cut pieces for each side. Cut strips on the crosswise grain of 42-inch wide fabric. (See Fabric Diagram 2 on Page 15.)

For Each Side

Center square:
Cut 16– 8" strips
Sub-cut 80 – 8" x 8"
(Sub-cuts are second cuts from the original strips. See Fabric Diagram 3, Page 15.)

Triangles (front side only):
Cut 16– 4" strips
Sub-cut 160– 4" x 4"

Rectangle 1:	Cut 12– 8" strips Sub-cut 160– 3" x 8"
Rectangle 2:	Cut 12– 10" strips Sub-cut 160– 3" x 10"
Rectangle 3:	Cut 4– 10" strips Sub-cut 40– 4" x 10"
Rectangle 4:	Cut 2– 20" strips Sub-cut 20– 4" x 20"
Rectangle 5:	Cut 3– 20" strips Sub-cut 25– 4" x 20"
Rectangle 6:	Cut 1– 84" strip Sub-cut 6– 4" x 84"
Binding	Cut 10– 2½" strips

Batting Cutting Instructions

Center squares:
Cut 80– 6"x 6"

Rectangle 1:
Cut 160– 1" x 6"

Rectangle 2:
Cut 160– 1" x 8"

Rectangle 3:
Cut 40– 2" x 8"

Rectangle 4:
Cut 20– 2" x 18"

Rectangle 5:
Cut 25– 2" x 18"

Rectangle 6:
Cut 6– 2" x 82"

*Betty's Advice:
When cutting the batting, cut longest pieces of batting first, and label your cut pieces.*

Tick-Tack-Toe King (25 blocks – 102" x 102")

Fabric Cutting Instructions

Cut carefully to ensure you have an adequate amount of fabric. Label your cut pieces for each side. Cut strips on the crosswise grain of 42-inch wide fabric. (See Fabric Diagram 2 on Page 15.)

For Each Side

Center square:
Cut 20– 8" strips
Sub-cut 100 – 8" x 8"
(Sub-cuts are second cuts from the original strips. See Fabric Diagram 3, Page 15.)

Triangles (front side only):
Cut 20– 4" strips
Sub-cut 200– 4" x 4"

Rectangle 1: Cut 15– 8" strips
Sub-cut 200– 3" x 8"

Rectangle 2: Cut 15– 10" strips
Sub-cut 200– 3" x 10"

Rectangle 3: Cut 5– 10" strips
Sub-cut 50– 4" x 10"

Rectangle 4: Cut 3– 20" strips
Sub-cut 25– 4" x 20"

Rectangle 5: Cut 3– 20" strips
Sub-cut 30– 4" x 20"

Rectangle 6: Cut 1– 104" strip
Sub-cut 6– 4" x 104"

Binding Cut 11– 2½" strips

Batting Cutting Instructions

Center squares:
Cut 100– 6"x 6"

Rectangle 1:
Cut 200– 1" x 6"

Rectangle 2:
Cut 200– 1" x 8"

Rectangle 3:
Cut 50– 2" x 8"

Rectangle 4:
Cut 25– 2" x 18"

Rectangle 5:
Cut 30– 2" x 18"

Rectangle 6:
Cut 6– 2" x 102"

Betty's Advice: When cutting the batting, cut longest pieces of batting first, and label your cut pieces.

All Sizes of Tick-Tack-Toe

Quilting Instructions

Insert quilting needle into your sewing machine. For best results, use a walking foot or even-feed foot when quilting.

Stitch suggestion: Use a 3.5 mm length straight stitch.

Thread suggestion: Match thread to the fabric for each side.

Center squares:

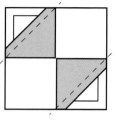

1. Layer fabric and batting. With back fabric right-side down, place batting in center and place front fabric right side up.

2. Press layers together with steam.

Front-Side Triangles:

Note: Work on four center squares at a time, and label them. When assembled, four center squares will make one unit block.

1. Mark a diagonal line on wrong side of 4" squares.

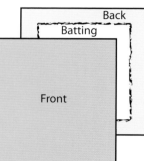

2. With right sides together, place 4" squares on top of front-side center squares so that outside edges line up and diagonal lines extend across corners of center squares, as indicated on diagrams in next column.

3. Stitch on diagonals, through all layers.

4. Trim the 4" squares and front-side fabric (top two layers) ¼" from the diagonal lines, as indicated on diagrams. (Do not cut batting or back side.)

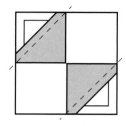
Top Left

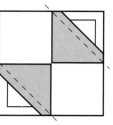
Top Right

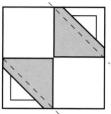
Bottom Left

Bottom Right

5. Press triangles toward corners, so that right side of fabric is seen.

Stitch suggestion: A zigzag 0.5 mm wide and 3.0 mm long will give the appearance of hand quilting, looking a little wobbly.

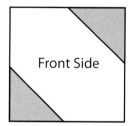
Front Side

6. Place edge of presser foot along seam of triangle and quilt a diagonal row.

7. Channel stitch another row one presser-foot width away from the previous quilting.

8. Repeat rows of diagonal channel stitching, alternating directions to compensate for fabric shifting (total of five rows next to each triangle.)

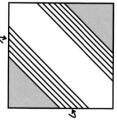

9. Complete steps 6 through 8 on other center squares with triangles.

Rectangles 1 & 2:

1. Pair up front sides and back sides.

2. Layer fabric and batting. With back fabric right-side down, place one layer of batting in center and place front fabric right side up.

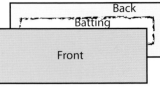

3. Press layers together with steam.

4. Place Adhesive Quilting Guide 1⅜" to the right of sewing machine needle.

5. Quilt down each side of the rectangles (total of two rows per rectangle).

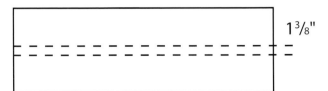

Rectangles 3 through 6:

1. Pair up front sides and back sides.

2. Layer fabric and batting. With back fabric right-side down, place one layer of batting in center and place front fabric right side up.

3. Press layers together with steam.

4. Place Adhesive Quilting Guide 2" to the right of sewing machine needle.

5. Quilt down the middle of each rectangle.

6. Channel stitch a row one presser-foot width away from the previous quilting.

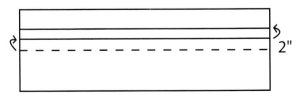

7. Channel stitch another row one presser-foot width away, alternating directions.

8. Channel stitch other half of rectangle in same manner (total of five rows).

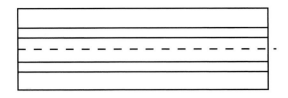

Assembly Instructions

Insert topstitch needle into your sewing machine. Seam allowances will be finished on the front side using Highway and One-Way Street procedures.

Note: Use a 1" seam allowance when sewing your quilted pieces together.

Thread suggestion: Variegated 40-weight cotton on top and variegated 50-weight cotton in bobbin.

1. With back sides together, sew Rectangle 1 to sides of center squares. Sew through all fabric layers.

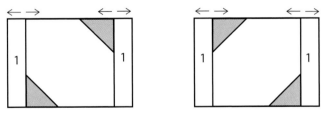

2. Press seams open on front side; then press the back side.

3. Finish seams using the Highway procedure. (See Techniques, Page 21.)

4. With back sides together, sew Rectangle 2 to the top and bottom of center squares.

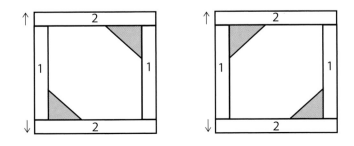

5. Press the back side; then press seam allowances on front side toward the outside edges.

6. Finish seams using the One-Way Street procedure. (See Techniques, Page 22.)

Note: Next you will add a sashing to connect the center square blocks.

7. With back sides together, sew Rectangle 3 to right-hand side of two center squares, as shown in diagram.

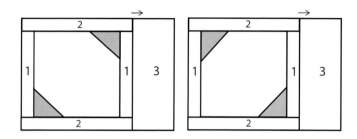

8. Press the back side; then press seam allowances on front side toward Rectangle 3.

9. Finish seams using the One-Way Street procedure.

10. With back sides together, sew Rectangle 3 to your mirror-image center squares, as shown in diagrams below and at top of next column. Be sure to align intersections. (See Techniques, Page 23.)

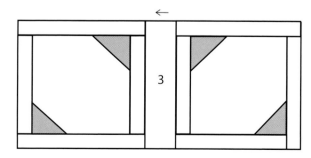

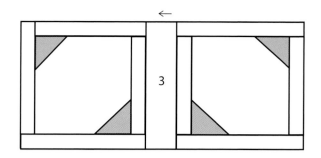

11. Press the back side; then press seam allowances on front side toward Rectangle 3.

12. Finish seams using the One-Way Street procedure.

13. With back sides together, sew Rectangle 4 to the bottom of the upper unit blocks, as shown in diagram.

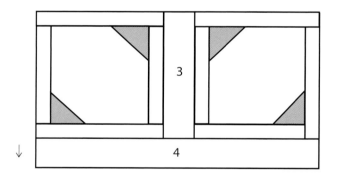

14. Press the back side; then press seam allowances on front side toward Rectangle 4.

15. Finish seams using the One-Way Street procedure.

16. With back sides together, sew upper and lower block units together, as shown in diagram on next page. Be sure to align intersections.

17. Press the back side; then press seam allowances on front side toward Rectangle 4.

18. Finish seams using the One-Way Street procedure.

19. Refer to finished quilt diagram on Page 102 to help you complete your quilt.

20. With back sides together, sew Rectangle 5 to connect your blocks into rows.

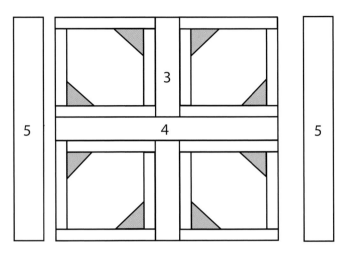

21. Press the back side; then press seam allowances on front side toward Rectangle 5.

22. Finish seam using the One-Way Street procedure.

23. With back sides together, sew Rectangle 6 to connect your rows.

24. Press the back side; then press seam allowances on front side toward Rectangle 6.

25. Finish seam using the One-Way Street procedure.

Applying Binding:

1. Trim ⅝" from raw edges of project, leaving a ⅜" seam allowance on all sides.

2. Apply binding. (For instructions, see Binding section at end of this book.)

Front side of Finished Tick-Tack-Toe Quilt in Various Sizes
(Back side has no triangles.)

Red lines indicate the different sizes of quilts, from a throw to a king-size version.
Make the size that suits your needs. Specific sizes are listed on Pages 90 and 91.

Two Little Tots Baby Quilt
(39"x 44")

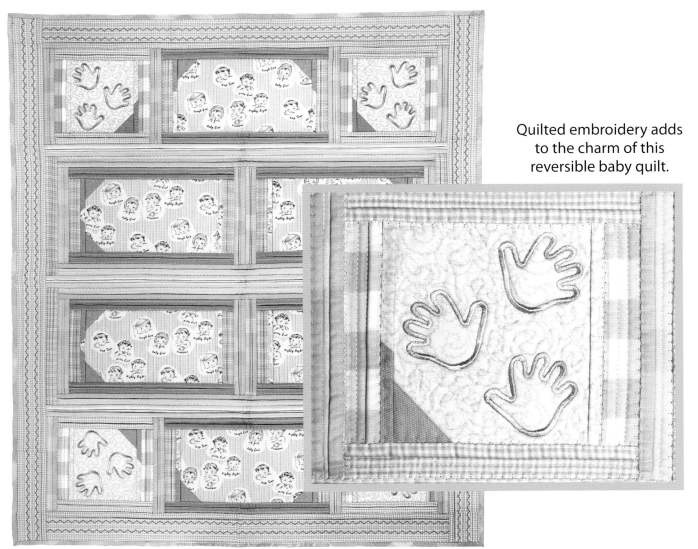

Quilted embroidery adds to the charm of this reversible baby quilt.

Front side of Two Little Tots Baby Quilt. (See back side on Page 104.)

Yardage Requirements
(Based on 42-inch wide fabric)

Front Side

Center rectangles:	½ yd. baby print
Background squares:	¼ yd. white
Triangles:	¼ yd. medium pink solid
Rectangle 1:	¼ yd. large pink/ white check
Rectangle 2:	¼ yd. beige/ pink plaid
Rectangle 3:	⅜ yd. small pink/ white check
Rectangle 4:	½ yd. medium pink stripe
Rectangle 5:	⅝ yd. large pink/ blue plaid
Rectangle 6:	⅜ yd. light pink stripe
Rectangle 7:	⅜ yd. pink/yellow plaid
Rectangle 8:	⅜ yd. white/pink stripe
Border:	⅝ yd. small pink/ white check

More yardage on Page 104

Back side of Two Little Tots Baby Quilt.

Back Side

Center rectangles: ½ yd. baby print

Background squares: ¼ yd. beige

Triangles: ¼ yd. medium blue solid

Rectangle 1: ¼ yd. large yellow/white check

Rectangle 2: ¼ yd. small yellow/white check

Rectangle 3: ⅜ yd. small blue/white check

Rectangle 4: ½ yd. medium blue stripe

Rectangle 5: ⅝ yd. small beige/white check

Rectangle 6: ⅜ yd. light yellow stripe

Rectangle 7: ⅜ yd. pink/blue plaid

Rectangle 8: ⅜ yd. yellow/white stripe

Border: ⅝ yd. small blue/white check

Binding

⅜ yd. large pink/blue plaid

Batting

Cotton Theory Batting, 18" x 108"

Fabric Cutting Instructions

Cut carefully to ensure you have an adequate amount of fabric. Label your cut pieces for each side. Cut strips on the crosswise grain of 42-inch wide fabric. (See Fabric Diagram 2 on Page 15.)

For Each Side

Center rectangles:
Cut 2– 8" strips
Sub-cut 6– 8" x 14"
(Sub-cuts are second cuts from the original strips. See Fabric Diagram 3 on Page 15.)

Background squares:
Cut 1– 8" strip
Sub-cut 4– 8" x 8"

Triangles:
Cut 2– 4" strips
Sub-cut 16– 4" x 4"

Rectangle 1:
Cut 1– 8" strip
Sub-cut 8– 3" x 8"

Rectangle 2:
Cut 1– 8" strip
Sub-cut 12– 3" x 8"

Rectangle 3:
Cut 1– 10" strip
Sub-cut 8– 3" x 10"

Rectangle 4:
Cut 1– 16" strip
Sub-cut 12– 3" x 16"

Rectangle 5:
Cut 2– 10" strips
Sub-cut 16– 3" x 10"

Rectangle 6:
Cut 4– 3" strips
Sub-cut 4– 3" x 34"

Rectangle 7:
Cut 1– 12" strip
Sub-cut 4– 3" x 12"

Rectangle 8:
Cut 3– 3" strips
Sub-cut 3– 3" x 36"

Borders:
Cut 4– 4½" strips
Sub-cut 4– 4½" x 41"

Binding

Cut 4– 2½" strips

Batting Cutting Instructions

Center rectangles:
Cut 6– 6"x 12"

Background squares:
Cut 4– 6"x 6"

Rectangle 1:
Cut 8– 1" x 6"

Rectangle 2:
Cut 12– 1" x 6"

Rectangle 3:
Cut 8– 1" x 8"

Rectangle 4:
Cut 12– 1" x 14"

Rectangle 5:
Cut 16– 1" x 8"

Rectangle 6:
Cut 4– 1" x 32"

Rectangle 7:
Cut 4– 1" x 10"

Rectangle 8:
Cut 3– 1" x 34"

Borders:
Cut 4– 2½"" x 39"

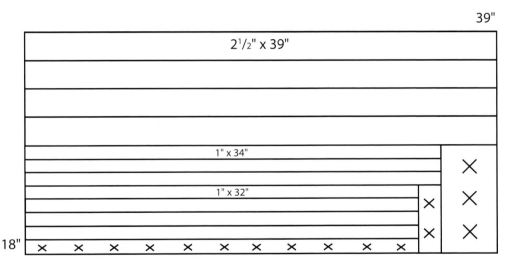

Cutting Diagram for Cotton Theory Batting (18" x 39")
X denotes batting that is not used

More diagrams on next page

Betty's Advice:
When cutting the batting, cut longest pieces of batting first, and label your cut pieces.

Quilted Embroidery Instructions

Insert embroidery needle into your sewing machine. Test-stitch a sample; increase upper tension, if neccessary. Use embroidery design of your choice, or follow design suggestion in this section. (For more quilted embroidery advice, see Techniques, Page 24.)

Thread suggestion: Light pink variegated 40-weight rayon on top and light blue 40-weight rayon in bobbin.

Design: OESD, Inc., Left Hand Print NV255 and OESD, Inc., Right Hand Print NV256. Available online from Oklahoma Embroidery Supply & Design, Inc. at www.EmbroideryOnline.com.

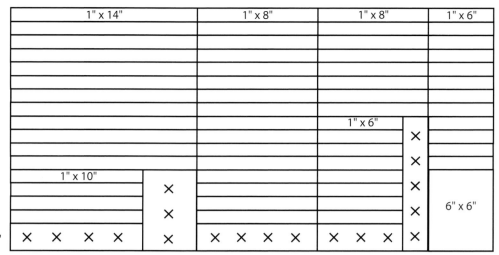

Cutting Diagram for Cotton Theory Batting (18" x 36")

Cutting Diagram for Cotton Theory Batting (18" x 30")

Background squares:

1. Layer fabric and batting. With back fabric right-side down, place batting in center, and place front fabric right side up.

2. Press layers together with steam.

3. Put a layer of water-soluble stabilizer in machine embroidery hoop.

4. Place layered fabric and batting on top of stabilizer.

5. Machine baste into place.

6. Embroider three hand prints (outline only) within a 5" to 5½" diameter on two background squares, embroidering through all layers.

OESD, Inc., Left Hand Print NV255 and Right Hand Print NV256 (outline only)

7. For remaining two background squares, mirror-image the embroidery design and repeat steps 1 through 6 to embroider.

8. Remove basting.

9. Dissolve stabilizer with water.

Quilting Instructions

Insert quilting needle into your sewing machine. For best results, use a walking foot or even-feed foot when quilting.

Stitch suggestion: Use a zigzag 3.0 mm long and .05 mm wide.

Thread suggestion: Match thread to the fabric for each side.

Center Rectangles:

1. Layer fabric and batting. With back fabric right-side down, place 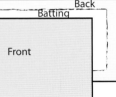 batting in center and place front fabric right side up.

2. Press layers together with steam.

3. Mark a vertical line 7" from one of the short sides of the center rectangle. This is the middle of the rectangle.

4. Quilt down the middle.

5. Channel-stitch another row one presser-foot width away from the previous quilting.

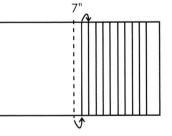

6. Repeat rows of channel stitching to within 1⅜" from edge of fabric, alternating directions to compensate for fabric shifting.

Note: Because presser-foot widths vary, the number of quilting rows will vary.

7. Channel-stitch the other half of the center rectangle in the same manner.

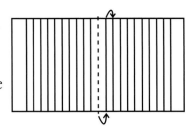

8. Repeat steps 1 through 7 for remaining center rectangles.

Rectangles 1 through 8:

1. Pair up front sides and back sides.

2. Layer fabric and batting. With back fabric right-side down, place one layer of batting in center and place front fabric right side up.

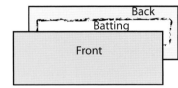

3. Press layers together with steam.

4. Place Adhesive Quilting Guide 1⅜" to the right of sewing machine needle.

5. Quilt down each side of the rectangles (total of two rows per rectangle).

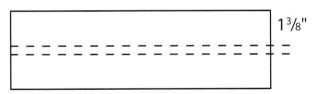

Borders:

Stitch: Lengthen straight stitch to 4.0 mm.

Thread suggestion: Light pink 40-weight rayon on top and medium blue 2 mm silk ribbon in bobbin.

Note: Loosen bobbin tension ¼ turn. Wind 5 yards of 2 mm silk ribbon on bobbin for each border piece. This ribbon can be machine wound.

1. Layer fabric and batting. With back fabric right-side down, place batting in center and place front fabric right side up.

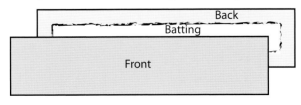

2. Press layers together with steam.

3. Place Adhesive Quilting Guide 2½" to the right of sewing machine needle.

4. Quilt down the middle of borders.

5. Place Adhesive Quilting Guide 1⅜" to the right of sewing machine needle.

6. Quilt down each side of the borders.

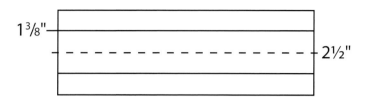

Thread change: Pastels variegated 40-weight cotton on top and medium pink 2 mm silk ribbon in bobbin. Wind 5 yards of ribbon on bobbin for each border piece.

7. Turn border over (back side up).

8. Using a light and airy decorative stitch (9 mm wide and 3 mm long), sew down the middle between the two channels of quilting.

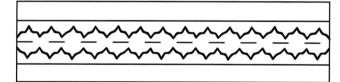

Front-Side Triangles:

Stitch: Use a 3.5 mm length straight stitch.

Thread suggestion: Cream 50-weight cotton on top and in bobbin.

1. Mark a diagonal line on wrong side of 4" squares.

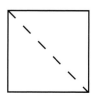

Betty's Advice: Label your quilted pieces to make assembly easier later.

2. With right sides together, place 4" square on top of front-side background square so that outside edges line up and diagonal line extends across corner of background square.

3. Stitch on the diagonal lines, through all layers.

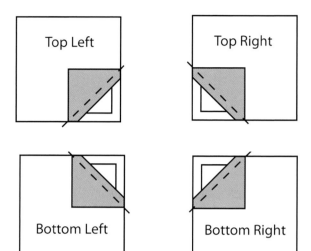

4. Trim the 4" squares and the front-side fabric (top two layers) ¼" from the diagonal lines, as indicated on diagram. (Do not cut batting or back side.)

5. Press triangles toward corners, so that right side of fabric is seen.

6. With right sides together, place 4" squares on top of front-side center rectangles so that outside edges line up and diagonal lines extend across corners of center squares, as indicated on diagram.

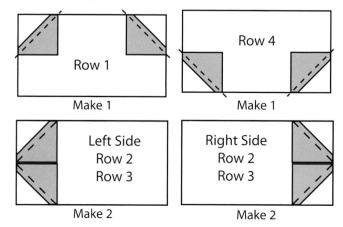

108

7. Stitch on the diagonal lines, through all layers.

8. Trim the 4" squares ¼" from the diagonal lines, as indicated on diagram. (Do not cut quilted center rectangle.)

9. Press triangles toward corners, so that right side of fabric is seen.

Back-Side Triangles:

Stitch suggestion: Use a 3.5 mm length straight stitch.

1. Mark a diagonal line on wrong side of 4" squares.

2. With right sides together, place 4" squares on top of back-side background squares in opposite corners from front side.

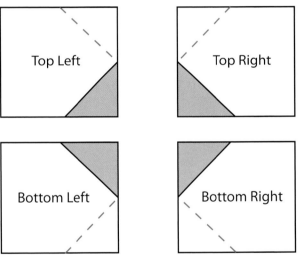

Red dotted lines indicate placement
of 4" squares for back side.

3. Stitch on the diagonal lines, through all layers.

4. Trim the 4" squares and the back-side fabric (top two layers) ¼" from the diagonal lines. (Do not cut batting and front-side fabric.)

5. Press triangles toward corners, so that right side of fabric is seen.

6. With right sides together, place 4" squares on top of back-side center

rectangles in opposite corners from front side.

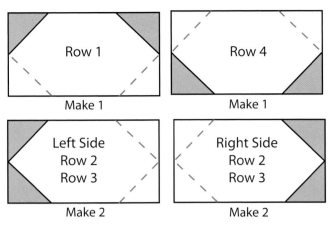

Red dotted lines indicate placement
of 4" squares for back side.

7. Stitch on the diagonal lines, through all layers.

8. Trim the 4" squares ¼" from the diagonal lines. (Do not cut quilted center rectangle.)

9. Press triangles toward corners, so that right side of fabric is seen.

Optional Quilting:

To balance the amount of quilting on the background squares and center rectangles, you may want to add more quilting to the squares.

1. Quilt in a free-motion meandering pattern around embroidered hands on the background squares. (Do not quilt triangles.)

2. Continue to quilt until you are within 1" of the raw edges of the squares.

109

Assembly Instructions

Insert topstitch needle into your sewing machine. Seam allowances will be finished on the front side using Highway and One-Way Street procedures.

Note: Use a 1" seam allowance when sewing your quilted pieces together.

Thread suggestion: Beige 50-weight cotton on top and light blue variegated 50-weight cotton in bobbin.

1. With back sides together, sew Rectangle 1 to sides of background squares, as shown in diagram. Sew through all fabric layers.

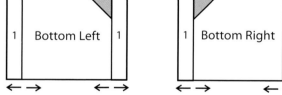

2. Press seams open on front side; then press the back side.

3. Finish seams using the Highway procedure. (See Techniques, Page 21.)

4. With back sides together, sew Rectangle 2 to the sides of center rectangles, as shown in diagram.

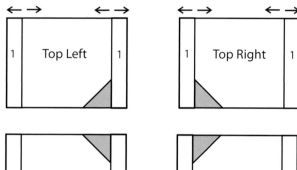

5. Press seams open on front side; then press the back side.

6. Finish seams using the Highway procedure.

7. With back sides together, sew Rectangle 3 to the top and bottom of background squares.

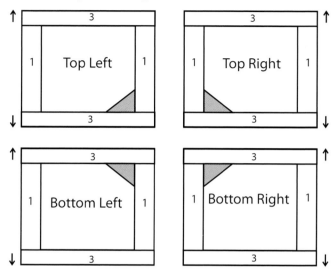

8. Press the back side; then press all seam allowances on front side toward the outside edges.

9. Finish seams using the One-Way Street procedure. (See Techniques, Page 22.)

10. With back sides together, sew Rectangle 4 to the top and bottom of center rectangles.

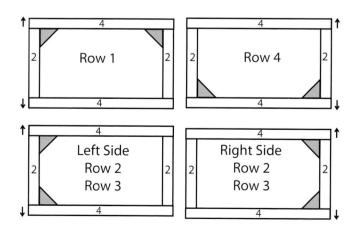

11. Press the back side; then press all seam allowances on front side toward the outside edges.

12. Finish seams using the One-Way Street procedure.

13. With back sides together, sew Rectangle 5 to sides of background square, as shown in diagram.

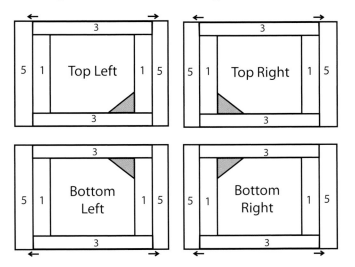

14. Press the back side; then press all seam allowances on front side toward the outside edges.

15. Finish seams using the One-Way Street procedure.

Connecting Background Squares and Center Rectangles:

1. With back sides together, sew background squares to both sides of center rectangles for Rows 1 and 4, as shown in diagrams. Be sure to align intersections. (See Techniques, Page 24.)

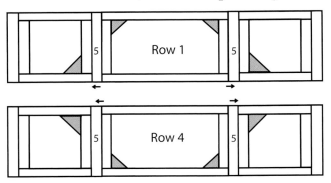

2. Press the back side; then press all seam allowances on front side toward Rectangle 5.

3. Finish seams using the One-Way Street procedure.

4. With back sides together, sew Rectangle 5 to the sides of center rectangles for Rows 2 and 3.

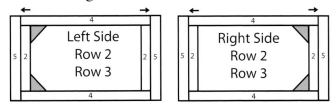

5. Press the back side; then press all seam allowances on front side toward outside edges.

6. Finish seams using the One-Way Street procedure.

7. With back sides together, sew sides of center rectangles together for Rows 2 and 3. Be sure to align intersections.

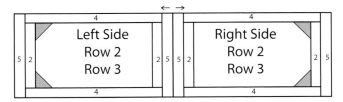

8. Press seams open on front side; then press the back side.

9. Finish seams using the Highway procedure.

10. With back sides together, sew Rectangle 6 to the top and bottom of Rows 2 and 3.

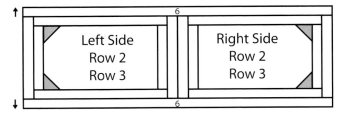

11. Press the back side; then press all seam allowances on front side toward the outside edges.

12. Finish seams using the One-Way Street procedure.

13. With back sides together, sew Rectangle 7 to sides of Rows 2 and 3.

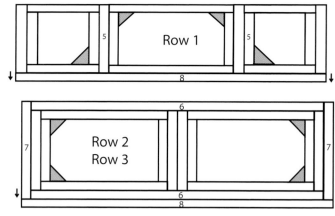

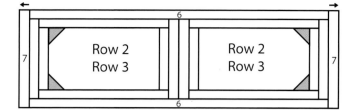

14. Press the back side; then press all seam allowances on front side toward the outside edges.

15. Finish seams using the One-Way Street procedure.

Applying Sashing:

1. With back sides together, sew Rectangle 8 to the bottom of Rows 1, 2 and 3.

2. Press the back side; then press all seam allowances on front side toward the outside edges.

3. Finish seams using the One-Way Street procedure.

Connecting the Rows:

1. With back sides together, sew Row 1 to Row 2.

2. Press the back side; then press all seam allowances on front side toward Rectangle 8.

3. Finish seam using the One-Way Street procedure.

4. Sew together Rows 2 and 3 and Rows 3 and 4 in the same manner. Finish seams using the One-Way Street procedure.

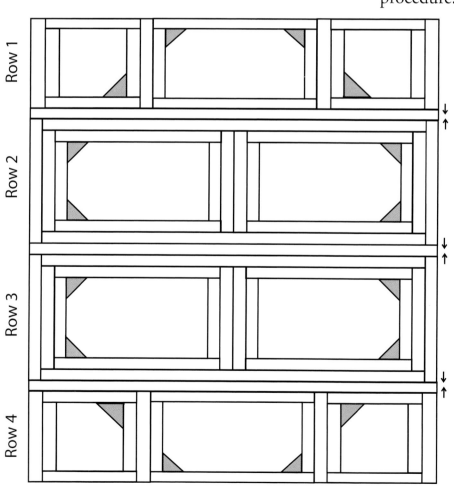

Applying Borders:

1. With back sides together, sew borders to sides of quilt.

2. Press the back side; then press all seam allowances on front side toward the outside edges.

3. Finish seams using the One-Way Street procedure.

4. With back sides together, sew borders to top and bottom of quilt.

5. Press the back side; then press all seam allowances on front side toward the outside edges.

6. Finish seams using the One-Way Street procedure.

Applying Binding:

1. Trim ⅝" from raw edges of project, leaving a ⅜" seam allowance on all sides.

2. Apply binding. (For instructions, see Binding section at end of this book.)

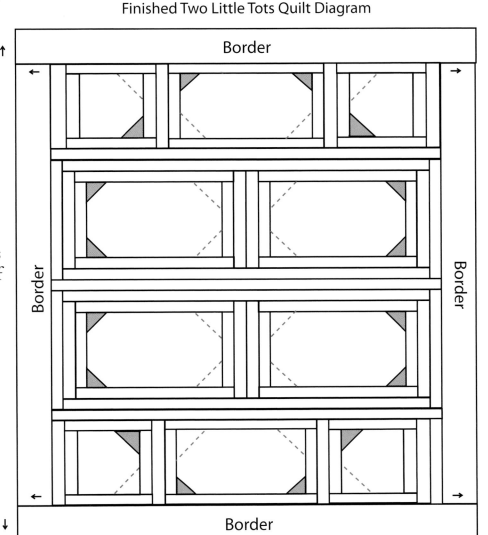

Finished Two Little Tots Quilt Diagram

Red dotted lines indicate placement of triangles on back side of quilt.

This Two Little Tots baby ensemble includes a quilt, pillow and bath mat, all made with Cotton Theory quilting techniques. All items are reversible. Instructions begin on Page 103 for the quilt, Page 115 for the pillow and Page 120 for the bath mat.

Two Little Tots Pillow
(19"x 13")

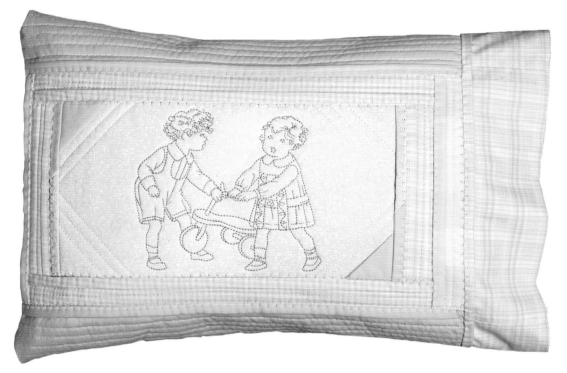

Like all Cotton Theory projects, this pillow cover is reversible. The other side is made in shades of blue, and the embroidery is a blue mirror-image of the front.

Yardage Requirements

(Based on 42-inch wide fabric)

This project uses fat quarters and fat eighths of fabric. For a definition, please turn to Page 14.

Front Side

Center rectangle:	Fat quarter ivory
Triangles:	Fat eighth pink
Rectangle 1:	Fat quarter pink/tan plaid
Rectangle 2:	Fat quarter pink/white check
Rectangle 3:	Fat quarter pink/blue/yellow plaid
Backing:	⅝ yd. pink pinstripe

Back Side

Center rectangle:	Fat quarter beige
Triangles:	Fat eighth blue
Rectangle 1:	Fat quarter yellow/white plaid
Rectangle 2:	Fat quarter blue/beige check
Rectangle 3:	Fat quarter yellow/white check
Backing:	⅝ yd. blue pinstripe

Casing

¼ yd. pink/blue plaid

Batting

Cotton Theory Batting, 18" x 32"

Fabric Cutting Instructions

Label your cut pieces for each side. Cut strips on the crosswise grain of fabric. (See Fabric Diagram 2 on Page 15.)

For Each Side

Center rectangle:
Cut 1– 8" strip
Sub-cut 1 – 8" x 14"
(Sub-cuts are second cuts from the original strips. See Fabric Diagram 3. Page 15.)

Triangles:
Cut 2– 4" x 4"

Rectangle 1:
Cut 1– 8" strip
Sub-cut 2– 3" x 8"

Rectangle 2:
Cut 1– 16" strip
Sub-cut 2– 3" x 16"

Rectangle 3:
Cut 1– 10" strip
Sub-cut 2– 3" x 10"

Backing:
Cut 1– 18" strip
Sub-cut 1– 18" x 20"

Casing
Cut 1– 8" strip
Sub-cut 1– 8" x 26½"

Batting Cutting Instructions

Center rectangle:
Cut 1– 6" x 12"

Rectangle 1:
Cut 2– 1" x 6"

Rectangle 2:
Cut 2– 1" x 14"

Rectangle 3:
Cut 2– 1" x 8"

Backing:
Cut 1– 16" x 18"

X denotes batting that is not used

Quilted Embroidery Instructions

Insert embroidery needle into your sewing machine. Test-stitch a sample; increase upper tension, if neccessary. Use embroidery design of your choice, or follow design suggestion in this section. (For more quilted embroidery advice, see Techniques, Page 24.)

Thread suggestion: Pink 40-weight rayon on top and blue 40-weight rayon in bobbin.

Design: Cactus Punch Quilting Vol. 4, "Mine!" design, enlarged to fit a 6" x 12" stitch field. Designs available through local sewing machine dealers.

Center Rectangle:

1. Layer fabric and batting. With back fabric right-side down, place 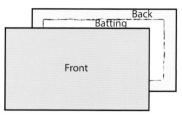 batting in center, and place front fabric right side up.

2. Press layers together with steam.

3. Place layered fabric and batting in machine embroidery hoop.

4. Embroider design in rectangle, embroidering through all layers.

Mine!
(from Cactus Punch Quilting Vol. 4)

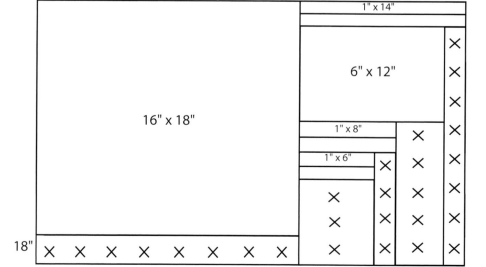

Cutting Diagram for Cotton Theory Batting (18" x 32")

Quilting Instructions

Insert quilting needle into your sewing machine. For best results, use a walking foot or even-feed foot when quilting.

Front-Side Triangles:

Stitch: Use a 3.5 mm length straight stitch.

Thread suggestion: Match thread to the fabric for each side.

1. Mark a diagonal line on wrong side of 4" squares.

2. With right sides together, place 4" squares on top of front-side center rectangle so that outside edges line up and diagonal lines extend across corners.

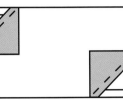

3. Stitch on the diagonal lines, through all layers.

4. Trim the 4" squares and the front-side fabric (top two layers) ¼" from the diagonal lines, as indicated on diagram. (Do not cut batting or back side.)

5. Press triangles toward corners, so that right side of fabric is seen.

Back-Side Triangles:

Stitch: Use a 3.5 mm long straight stitch.

1. Mark a diagonal line on wrong side of 4" squares.

2. With right sides together, place 4" squares on top of back-side center rectangle in opposite corners from front side.

3. Stitch on the diagonal lines, through all layers.

Red dotted lines indicate placement of 4" squares for back side.

4. Trim the 4" squares and the back-side fabric (top two layers) ¼" from the diagonal lines. (Do not cut batting and front-side fabric.)

5. Press triangles toward corners, so that right side of fabric is seen.

Stitch suggestion: A zigzag 0.5mm wide and 3.0 mm long will give the appearance of hand quilting, looking a little wobbly.

6. On front side of center rectangle, place edge of presser foot along seam lines of triangles and quilt one row.

7. Channel-stitch another row toward the middle, one presser-foot width away from the previous quilting.

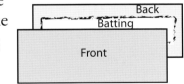

Red dotted lines indicate triangles on back side.

Rectangles 1 through 3:

1. Layer fabric and batting. With back fabric right-side down, place one layer of batting in center, and place front fabric right side up.

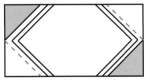

2. Press layers together with steam.

3. Place Adhesive Quilting Guide 1⅜" to the right of sewing machine needle.

4. Quilt down each side of the rectangles (total of two rows per rectangle).

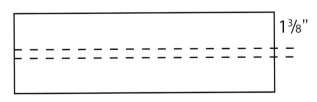

Backing:

1. Layer fabric and batting. With back fabric right-side down, place batting in center, and place front fabric right side up.

2. Press layers together with steam.

3. Mark a horizontal line 10" from short side of rectangle. (This is the middle.)

4. Quilt down the middle.

5. Channel-stitch another row one presser-foot width away from the previous quilting.

6. Repeat rows of channel stitching to within 1⅜" from edge of fabric,

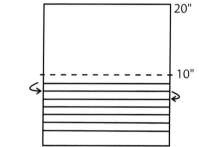

alternating directions to compensate for fabric shifting.

Note: Because presser-foot widths vary, the number of quilting rows will vary.

7. Channel-stitch the other half of the backing in the same manner.

Assembly Instructions

Insert topstitch needle into your sewing machine. Seam allowances will be finished on the front side using Highway and One-Way Street procedures.

Note: Use a 1" seam allowance when sewing your quilted pieces together.

1. With back sides together, sew Rectangle 1 to sides of center rectangle. Sew through all fabric layers.

2. Press seams open on front side; then press the back side.

3. Finish seams using the Highway procedure. (See Techniques, Page 21.)

4. With back sides together, sew Rectangle 2 to the top and bottom of center rectangle.

5. Press the back side; then press all seam allowances on front side toward the outside edges.

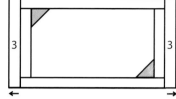

6. Finish seams using the One-Way Street procedure.

7. With back sides together, sew Rectangle 3 to the sides of center rectangle.

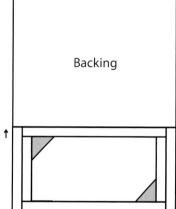

8. Press the back side; then press all seam allowances on front side toward the outside edges.

9. Finish seams using the One-Way Street procedure. (See Techniques, Page 22.)

Applying Backing:

1. With back sides together, sew backing to top of center rectangle.

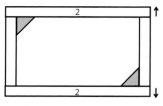

2. Press the back side; then press seam allowances on front side toward the backing.

3. Finish seams using the One-Way Street procedure.

4. With back sides together, sew backing to bottom of center rectangle, forming a tube.

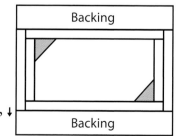

5. Press the back side; then press seam allowances on front side toward the backing.

6. Finish seams using the One-Way Street procedure.

Applying Casing:

1. With right sides together, sew ends of casing together with a ¼" seam, forming a tube.

2. Press seam open.

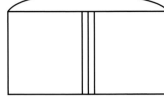

3. With wrong sides together, fold casing in half, forming a shorter tube that has the right side of the fabric on the outside.

4. Press casing.

5. With back sides together and raw edges even, sew casing to back side of pillow with a 1" seam.

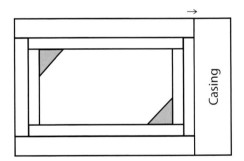

6. Press the back side; then press seam allowances on front side toward casing.

7. Finish seam using the One-Way Street procedure.

Completing the Self-Binding:

Note: The self-binding closure will be on the back side.

1. Center the embroidery and press the tube of fabric to crease edges of the backing.

2. With front sides together, sew the end of the tube that is opposite the casing. Use a 1" seam allowance, and backstitch at beginning and end.

3. Starting ¼" from each side of the pillow case, make a ¾" cut in the top two layers of the 1" seam allowance.

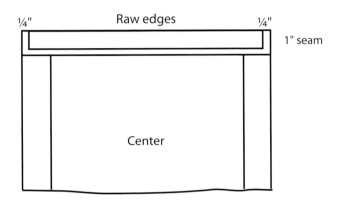

4. Trim the top two layers of the seam allowance down to ¼" across the width of the pillow case. (The remaining two seam allowances will be used to self-bind the end of the pillow.)

5. Finish seam using the One-Way Street procedure. Backstitch at beginning and end.

Two Little Tots Bath Mat

(18"x 34")

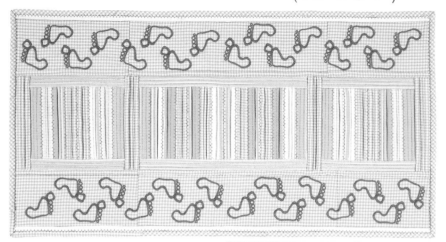

Front side of
Two Little Tots Bath Mat

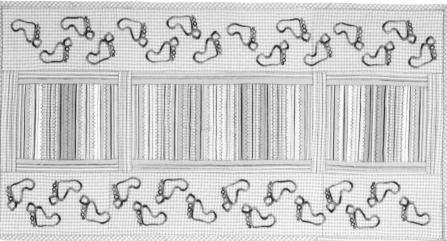

Back side of Two Little Tots Bath Mat

Yardage Requirements

(Based on 42-inch wide fabric)

Use medium-weight fabric, such as twill ticking.

Front Side

Center squares & center rectangle: ¼ yd. each of 4 assorted fabrics — pink, beige, white checks & stripes

Rectangles 1 & 2: ¼ yd. solid pink

Rectangles 3 & 4: ½ yd. beige stripe

Rectangle 5 & Border: 1⅛ yd. small pink/ white check

Back Side

Yardage for front side is enough for both sides, if you prefer to use the same colors. Pieces are then cut on the lengthwise grain.

Center squares & center rectangle: ¼ yd. each of 4 assorted fabrics — blue/beige/yellow checks & stripes

More yardage on next page

Rectangles 1 & 2:	¼ yd. solid blue
Rectangles 3 & 4:	½ yd. pink/blue stripe
Rectangle 5 & Border:	1⅛ yd. small blue/white check

Highway Binding

Flange:	¼ yd. white
Binding:	⅜ yd. beige check

Batting

Cotton Theory Batting, 18" x 34"

The reversible Two Little Tots Bath Mat has three-dimensional folds on both sides.

Fabric Cutting Instructions

Label your cut pieces for each side. Cut strips on the crosswise grain of 42-inch wide fabric. (See Fabric Diagram 2 on Page 15.)

Front Side

From the 4 assorted fabrics:
Cut 1– 8" strip each (total of 4)

> **Center squares:**
> Sub-cut 3 each 3" x 8" (total 12)
>
> **Center rectangle:**
> Sub-cut 3 each 3" x 8" (total 12)
> *(Sub-cuts are second cuts from the original strips. See Fabric Diagram 3, Page 15.)*

From the solid pink:
Cut 1– 8" strip

> **Rectangle 1:**
> Sub-cut 4– 3" x 8"
>
> **Rectangle 2:**
> Sub-cut 2– 3" x 8"

From the beige stripe:
Cut 1– 16" strip

> **Rectangle 4:**
> Sub-cut 2– 3" x 16"
>
> **Rectangle 3:**
> Sub-cut 4– 3" x 10"

From the small pink/white check:
Cut 1– 36" strip

> **Border:**
> Sub-cut 2– 7" x 36"
>
> **Rectangle 5:**
> Sub-cut 4– 3" x 10"

Back Side

From the 4 assorted fabrics:
Cut 1– 8" strip each (total 4)

> **Center squares:**
> Sub-cut 3 each 3" x 8" (total 12)
>
> **Center rectangle:**
> Sub-cut 3 each 3" x 8" (total 12)

From the solid blue:
Cut 1– 8" strip

> **Rectangle 1:**
> Sub-cut 4– 3" x 8"
>
> **Rectangle 2:**
> Sub-cut 2– 3" x 8"

From the pink/blue stripe:
Cut 1– 16" strip

> **Rectangle 4:**
> Sub-cut 2– 3" x 16"
>
> **Rectangle 3:**
> Sub-cut 4– 3" x 10"

From the small blue/white check:
Cut 1– 36" strip

> **Border:**
> Sub-cut 2– 7" x 36"
>
> **Rectangle 5:**
> Sub-cut 4– 3" x 10"

Highway Binding
From white:
Cut 2– 3" strips
Sub-cut 2– 3" x 36" (flange)

From beige check:
Cut 3– 3" strips (binding)

Batting Cutting Instructions

Label your cut pieces.

Center squares:
Cut 12– 1"x 6"

Center rectangle:
Cut 12– 1"x 6"

Rectangle 1:
Cut 4– 1" x 6"

Rectangle 2:
Cut 2– 1" x 6"

Rectangle 3:
Cut 4– 1" x 8"

Rectangle 4:
Cut 2– 1" x 14"

Rectangle 5:
Cut 4– 1" x 8"

Borders:
Cut 2– 5" x 34"

34"

5" x 34"

| | 1" x 14" | | 1" x 6" | 1" x 6" | 1" x 8" |
| 1" x 6" | 1" x 6" | 1" x 6" | | | |

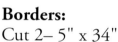

18"

Cutting Diagram for Cotton Theory Batting (18" x 34")

Quilting Instructions

Insert quilting needle into your sewing machine. For best results, use a walking foot or even-feed foot when quilting.

Stitch: Use a 3.5 mm length straight stitch.

Thread suggestion: Match thread to the fabric for each side.

Center Squares, Center Rectangle and Rectangles 1 through 5:

Note: When completed, the center squares will be made up of six quilted pieces sewn together, and the center rectangle will be 12 quilted pieces sewn together.

1. Pair up front sides and back sides.

2. Layer fabric and batting. With back fabric right-side down, place batting in center and place front fabric right side up.

Betty's Advice: Label your quilted pieces so you can assemble your project easily.

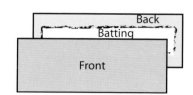

3. Press layers together with steam.

4. Place Adhesive Quilting Guide 1⅜" to the right of sewing machine needle.

5. Quilt down each side of the layered pieces (total of two rows per rectangle).

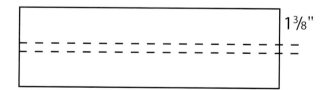

1⅜"

Quilted Embroidery Instructions

Insert embroidery needle into your sewing machine. Test-stitch a sample; increase upper tension, if neccessary. Use embroidery design of your choice, or follow design suggestion in this section. (For more quilted embroidery advice, see Techniques, Page 24.)

Thread suggestion: Light pink 50-weight cotton on top and light blue variegated 50-weight cotton in bobbin.

Design: OESD, Inc., Left Foot Print NV258 and OESD, Inc., Right Foot Print NV257. Available online from Oklahoma Embroidery Supply & Design, Inc. at www.EmbroideryOnline.com.

Borders:

1. Layer fabric and batting. With back fabric right-side down, place batting in center, and place front fabric right side up.

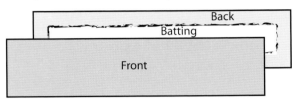

2. Press layers together with steam.

3. Put a layer of water-soluble stabilizer in machine embroidery hoop.

4. Place layered fabric and batting on top of stabilizer.

5. Machine baste into place.

6. Embroider four footprints (outline only) within an 8½" x 4" space, stitching through all layers.

7. Repeat Step 6, embroidering a total of four sets of footprints for each border.

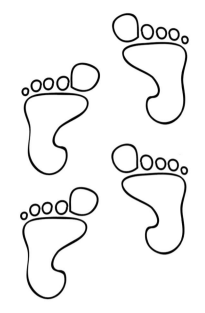

OESD, Inc., Left Foot Print NV258 and Right Foot Print NV257 (outline only). This illustrates one set of embroidered footprints.

8. Remove basting.

9. Dissolve stabilizer with water.

Assembly Instructions

Insert topstitch needle into your sewing machine. Seam allowances will be finished on the front side and the back side using Highway and One-Way Street procedures.

Note: Use a 1" seam allowance when sewing your quilted pieces together.

Thread suggestion: Pastels 40-weight cotton on top and in bobbin.

Center Squares and Center Rectangle:

1. Arrange pieces for center squares and center rectangle and identify them A,B, C, D, as shown in diagram.

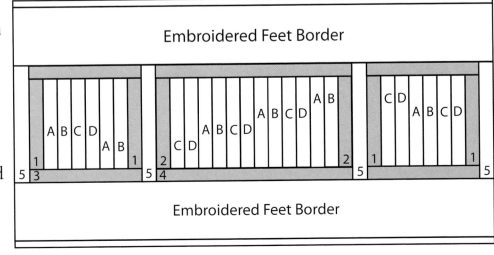

Note: In the diagrams, arrows pointing up indicate seam allowances finished on the front side; arrows pointing down indicate seam allowances finished on the back side.

2. With back sides together, sew B to A.

3. Press seams open on front side; then press the back side.

4. Finish seams on the front side using the Highway procedure. (See Techniques, Page 21.)

5. With front sides together, sew C to B.

6. Press seams open on back side; then press the front side.

7. Finish seams on the back side using the Highway procedure.

8. With back sides together, sew D to C.

9. Press seams open on front side; then press the back side.

10. Finish seams on the front side using the Highway procedure.

11. Follow the diagram and continue adding rectangles in the same manner, alternating the seam allowances on the back side and front side, as indicated by the arrows.

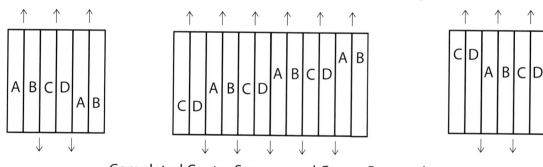

Completed Center Squares and Center Rectangle

Adding Rectangle 1 to Center Squares:

1. With front sides together, sew Rectangle 1 to sides of center squares.

2. Press seams open on back side; then press the front side.

3. Finish seams on the back side using the Highway procedure.

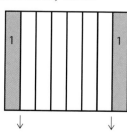

Adding Rectangle 2 to Center Rectangle:

1. With front sides together, sew Rectangle 2 to sides of center rectangle.

2. Press seams open on back side; then press the front side.

3. Finish seams on the back side using the Highway procedure.

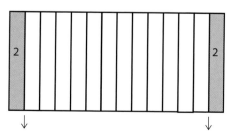

Rectangles 3 through 5:

1. With front sides together, sew Rectangle 3 to the top and bottom of center squares.

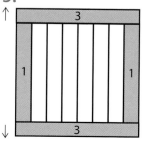

2. Press the front side; then press all seam allowances on back side toward the outside edges.

3. Finish seams on back side using the One-Way Street procedure. (See Techniques, Page 22.)

4. With front sides together, sew Rectangle 4 to the top and bottom of center rectangle.

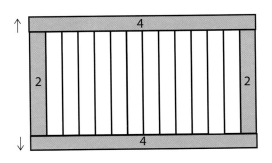

5. Press the front side; then press all seam allowances on back side toward outside edges.

6. Finish seams on back side using the One-Way Street procedure.

7. With back sides together, sew Rectangle 5 to the sides of center square.

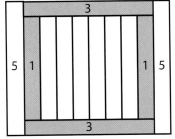

8. Press the back side; then press all seam allowances on front side toward the outside edges.

9. Finish seams on front side using the One-Way Street procedure.

Connecting the Centers:

1. With back sides together, sew center square to center rectangle to center square, as shown in diagram. Be sure to align intersections. (See Techniques, Page 23.)

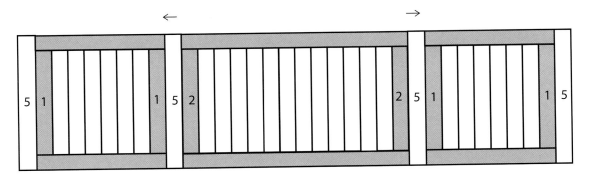

2. Press the back side; then press all seam allowances on front side toward Rectangle 5.

3. Finish seams on front side using the One-Way Street procedure.

Applying Borders:

1. With back sides together, sew borders to top and bottom of center unit.

2. Press the back side; then press all seam allowances on front side toward the border.

3. Finish seams on front side using the One-Way Street procedure.

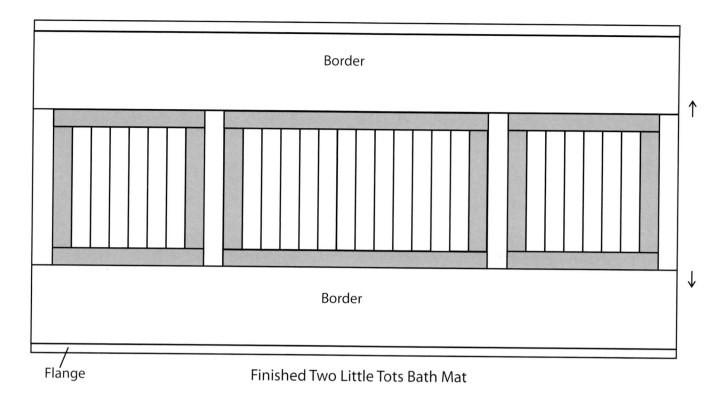

Flange   Finished Two Little Tots Bath Mat

Applying Highway Binding:

1. Trim ½" from raw edges of project, leaving a ½" seam allowance on all sides.

2. Apply Highway Binding. (For instructions, see Page 148 in Binding section at end of this book.)

Note: The flange should be applied only to the border sides of the bath mat, not to the short sides.

Two Dear Darling Daughters
Bed Quilt (87"x 103")

Turn the page to learn how to make this elegant, queen-size, reversible quilt.
The front side is shown here. The back side is on the next page.

Yardage Requirements

(Based on 42-inch wide fabric)

Front Side

Center squares:
1 yd. beige print

Center rectangles:
1½ yd. beige print

Triangles:
⅝ yd. green/gray batik

Rectangle 1:
¾ yd. small gold print

Rectangle 2:
¾ yd. second small gold print

Rectangle 3:
⅞ yd. small green print

Rectangle 4:
1½ yd. second small green print

Rectangle 5:
1¼ yd. third small gold print

Rectangle 6:
⅜ yd. fourth small gold print

Sashing 7:
1⅛ yd. third small green print

Sashing 8:
½ yd. second small gold print

Back side of Two Dear Darling Daughters Bed Quilt.

First border:
2⅛ yd. green/gray batik

Flange insert:
¾ yd. small barn red print

Second border:
2½ yd. barn red micro check

Third border:
⅞ yd. second small green print

Fourth border:
2¾ yd. beige print

Bias insert:
⅝ yd. small barn red print

Thread:
50 wt. cotton beige, gold, green.

40 wt. dark variegated (quilted embroidery)

40 wt. dark red variegated (topstitching)

2 mm variegated silk ribbon (thread can be used instead)

Back Side

Center squares:
1 yd. beige print

Center rectangles:
1½ yd. beige print

Triangles:
⅝ yd. dark blue batik

Rectangle 1:
¾ yd. dark red batik

More on next page

Rectangle 2:
¾ yd. dark mauve batik

Rectangle 3:
⅞ yd. medium blue batik

Rectangle 4:
1½ yd. dark purple batik

Rectangle 5:
1¼ yd. medium plum batik

Rectangle 6:
⅜ yd. dark pink batik

Sashing 7:
1⅛ yd. dark batik print

Sashing 8:
½ yd. dark mauve batik

First border:
2⅛ yd. dark purple batik

Second border:
2½ yd. beige print

Third border:
⅞ yd. dark batik print

Fourth border:
2¾ yd. medium plum batik

Thread:
50 wt. cotton dark red, plum, blue, purple

39 g dark purple variegated yarn (quilted embroidery) (thread can be used instead)

40 wt. rayon dark red (quilted embroidery)

40 wt. cotton dark purple variegated (topstitching)

39 g light beige variegated yarn (quilting) (thread can be used instead)

Single-Fold Bias Binding
⅝ yd. beige print

Batting
Cotton Theory Batting, 18" x 15 yd.

Fabric Cutting Instructions

Cut carefully to ensure you have an adequate amount of fabric. Label your cut pieces for each side. Cut strips on the crosswise grain of 42-inch wide fabric. (See Fabric Diagram 2 on Page 15.)

For Each Side

Center squares:
Cut 4– 8" strips
Sub-cut 16 – 8" x 8"
(Sub-cuts are second cuts from the original strips. See Fabric Diagram 3 on Page 15.)

Center rectangles:
Cut 6– 8" strips
Sub-cut 16– 8" x 14"

Triangles:
Cut 5– 4" strips
Sub-cut 48– 4" x 4"

Rectangle 1:
Cut 3– 8" strips
Sub-cut 32– 3" x 8"

Rectangle 2:
Cut 3– 8" strips
Sub-cut 32– 3" x 8"

Rectangle 3:
Cut 3– 10" strips
Sub-cut 32– 3" x 10"

Rectangle 4:
Cut 3– 16" strips
Sub-cut 32– 3" x 16"

Rectangle 5:
Cut 4– 10" strips
Sub-cut 44– 3" x 10"

Rectangle 6:
Cut 1– 10" strip
Sub-cut 12– 3" x 10"

Sashing 7:
Cut 1– 36" strip
Sub-cut 14– 3" x 36"

Sashing 8:
Cut 4– 3" strips (piece together)
Sub-cut 3– 3" x 57"
(Sashings connect sections of a quilt.)

First border:
Cut 1– 73" strip
Sub-cut 2– 8" x 73"
Sub-cut 2– 8" x 69"

Flange insert (front side):
Cut 8– 3" strips (piece together)
Sub-cut 2– 3" x 69"
Sub-cut 2– 3" x 85"

Second border:
Cut 1– 85" strip
Sub-cut 6– 3" x 85"
Sub-cut 6– 3" x 75"

Third border:
Cut 9– 3" strips (piece together)
Sub-cut 2– 3" x 91"
Sub-cut 2– 3" x 77"

Fourth border:
Cut 1– 93" strip
Sub-cut 2– 9" x 93"
Sub-cut 2– 9" x 91"

Bias insert (front side):
Cut 1– 20" strip
Sub-cut 2– 20" x 20" squares
Sub-cut 1¼" bias strips from squares (total of 400")
(See Page 145.)

Single-Fold Bias Binding

Cut 1– 20" strip
Sub-cut 2– 20" x 20" squares
Sub-cut 1½" bias strips from squares (total of 400")
(See Page 145.)

Batting Cutting Instructions

Center squares:
Cut 16– 6"x 6"

Center rectangles:
Cut 16– 6"x 12"

Rectangle 1:
Cut 32– 1" x 6"

Rectangle 2:
Cut 32– 1" x 6"

Rectangle 3:
Cut 32– 1" x 8"

Rectangle 4:
Cut 32– 1" x 14"

Rectangle 5:
Cut 44– 1" x 8"

Rectangle 6:
Cut 12– 1" x 8"

Sashing 7:
Cut 14– 1" x 34"

Sashing 8:
Cut 3– 1" x 55"

First border:
Cut 2– 6" x 71"
Cut 2– 6" x 67"

Second border:
Cut 6– 1" x 83"
Cut 6– 1" x 73"

Third border:
Cut 2– 1" x 89"
Cut 2– 1" x 75"

Fourth border:
Cut 2– 7" x 89"
Cut 2– 7" x 91"

Betty's Advice: Cut longest pieces of batting first. Label your cut pieces.

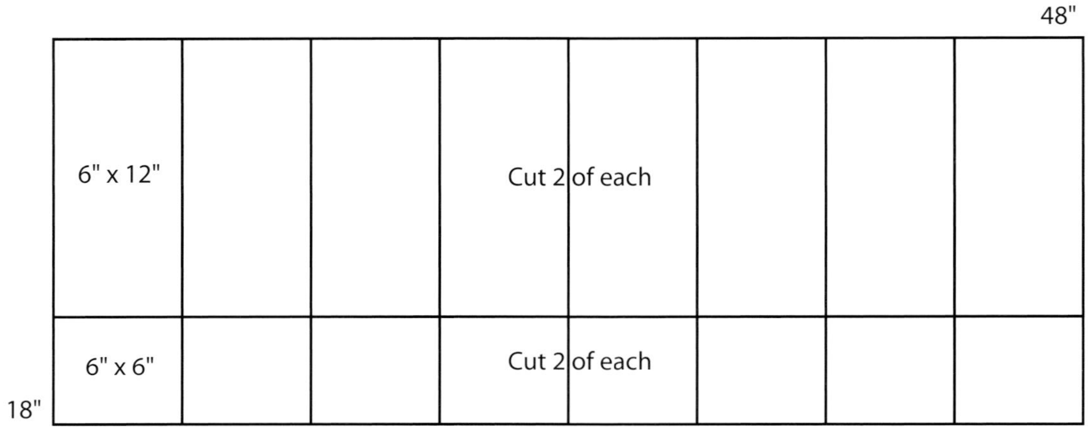

48"

6" x 12"			Cut 2 of each				
6" x 6"			Cut 2 of each				

18"

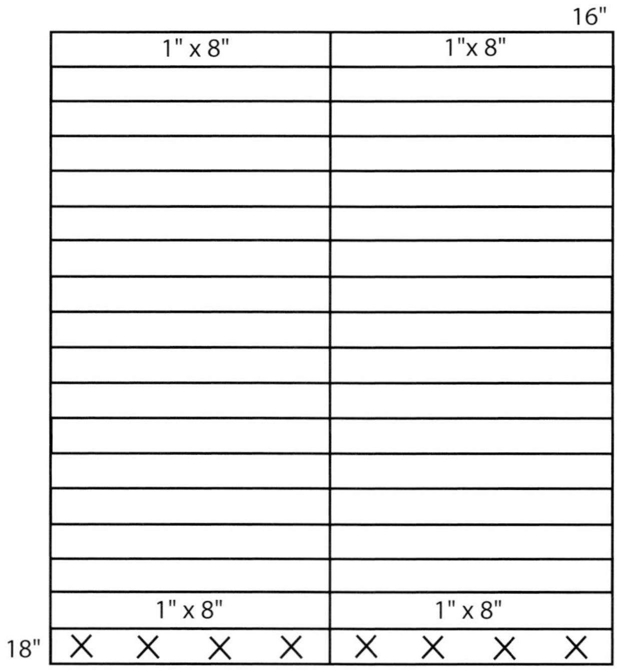

16"

1" x 8"	1"x 8"
1" x 8"	1" x 8"
X X X X	X X X X

18"

X denotes batting that is not used

Cutting Diagrams for Cotton Theory Batting (18" x 48" twice) (18" x 16")

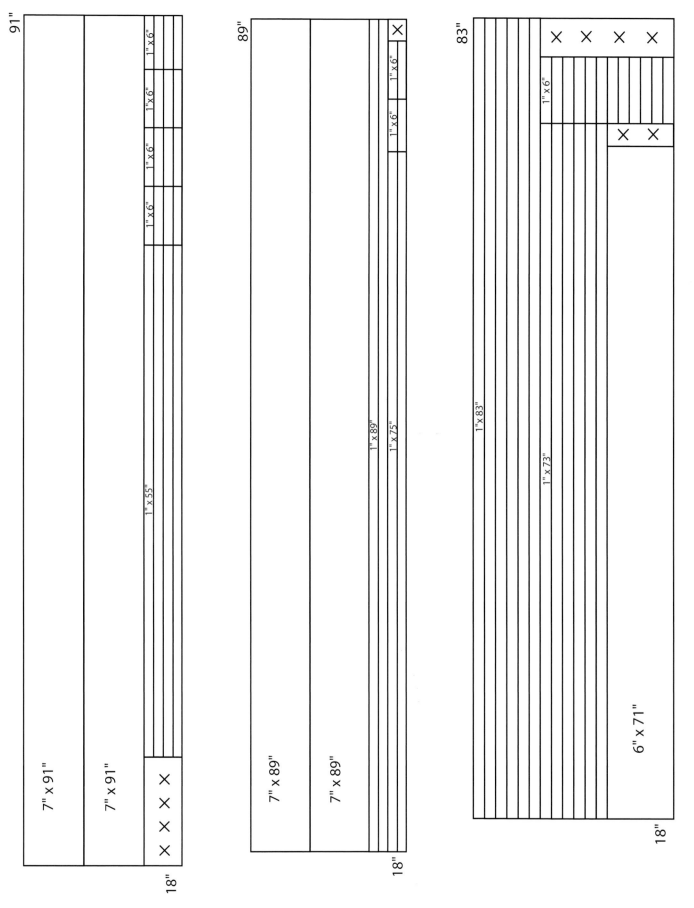

Cutting Diagrams for Cotton Theory Batting (18" x 91") (18" x 89") (18" x 83")

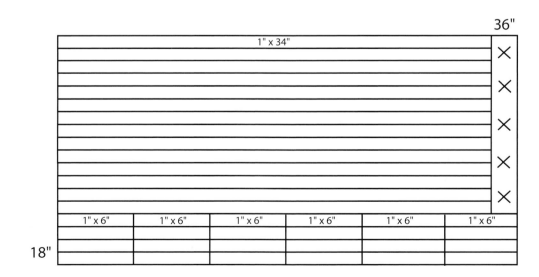

52"

1" x 14"	1" x 14"	1" x 8"	1" x 8"	1" x 8"

18"

1" x 6"	1" x 6"	✕	1" x 6"	1" x 6"	✕

71"

6" x 71"
6" x 67"
6" x 67"

18"

36"

1" x 34"

1" x 6"	1" x 6"	1" x 6"	1" x 6"	1" x 6"	1" x 6"

18"

Cutting Diagrams for Cotton Theory Batting (18" x 52") (18" x 71") (18" x 36")

Quilted embroidery and bobbin work add eye-catching details to the Two Dear Darling Daughters Bed Quilt.

Quilted Embroidery Instructions

Insert embroidery needle into your sewing machine. Test-stitch a sample; increase upper tension, if neccessary. Use embroidery design of your choice, or follow design suggestion in this section. (For more quilted embroidery advice, see Techniques, Page 24.)

Center Squares:

Thread suggestion: Dark red 40-weight rayon on top and 2 mm variegated silk ribbon in bobbin.

Design: Pfaff 354 Fine Line Art, Design 3 (outline only), resized to fit 6" x 6". Design available through Pfaff dealers.

Note: By embroidering center squares upside down (back-side fabric up), you can feature bobbin work on the front of your quilt.

1. Layer fabric and batting. With back fabric right-side down, place batting in center, and place front fabric right side up.

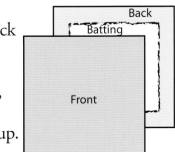

2. Press layers together with steam.

3. Put a layer of water-soluble stabilizer in machine embroidery hoop.

4. Place layered fabric and batting on hoop upside down, with back fabric facing right side up.

5. Machine baste into place.

6. Embroider eight center squares with design, stitching through all layers.

Pfaff 354 Fine Line Art, Design 3 (outline only)

Mirror image of Pfaff 354 Fine Line Art, Design 3 (outline only)

7. Mirror-image embroidery design and embroider eight more center squares.

8. Remove basting.

9. Dissolve stabilizer with water.

Center Rectangles:

Thread suggestion: Dark variegated 40-weight cotton on top and 39 g dark purple variegated yarn in bobbin.

Design: Pfaff 354 Fine Line Art, Design 6 (Steps 2 and 3 only), resized to fit 6" x 12". Design available through Pfaff dealers.

Note: It may not be necessary to use water-soluble stabilizer in the machine embroidery hoop if the 8" x 14" rectangles fit snugly in the hoop.

1. Layer fabric and batting. With back fabric right-side down, place batting in center, and place front fabric right side up.

2. Press layers together with steam.

3. Place layered fabric and batting in machine embroidery hoop.

4. Embroider 12 center rectangles, stitching through all layers.

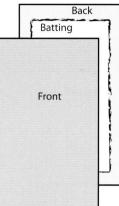

Pfaff 354 Fine Line Art, Design 6 (Steps 2 and 3 only)

Mirror image of Pfaff 354 Fine Line Art, Design 6 (Steps 2 and 3 only)

5. Mirror-image the embroidery design and embroider four more center rectangles.

Quilting Instructions

Insert quilting needle into your sewing machine. For best results, use a walking foot or even-feed foot when quilting.

Stitch suggestion: Use a 3.5 mm length straight stitch.

Thread suggestion: Match thread to the fabric for each side.

Front-Side and Back-Side Triangles:

1. Arrange center squares and center rectangles as shown in the diagrams here and on next page. Add triangles by following instructions on the next page.

Placement of center squares and center rectangles, Rows 1 through 6

X marks placement of mirror-image embroidery

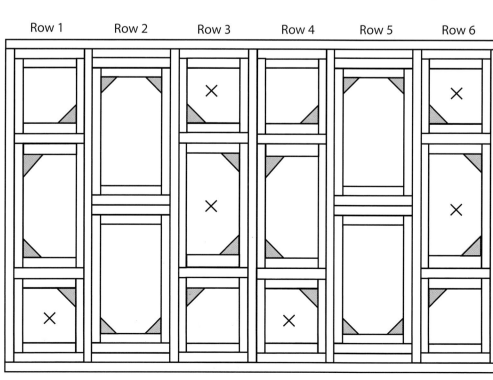

Row 1   Row 2   Row 3   Row 4   Row 5   Row 6

Placement of center squares and center rectangles, Rows 7 through 12

X marks placement of mirror-image embroidery

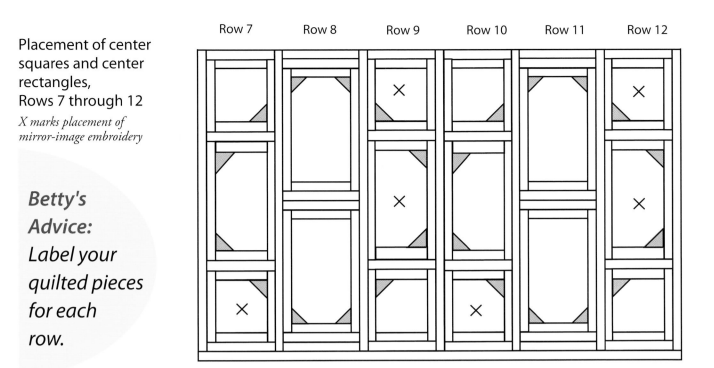

Row 7 | Row 8 | Row 9 | Row 10 | Row 11 | Row 12

Betty's Advice: *Label your quilted pieces for each row.*

2. Mark a diagonal line on wrong sides of front-side 4" fabric squares (for triangles).

Note: You will be sewing front-side and back-side triangles at the same time.

3. With right sides together, place 4" squares on fronts and backs of center squares and center rectangles so that outside edges line up and diagonal line extends across corner. (See quilt diagram for placement.)

4. Stitch on the diagonal line, through all layers.

5. Trim the 4" squares and the front-side and back-side fabrics ¼" from the diagonal line, as shown in diagram. (Do not cut batting.)

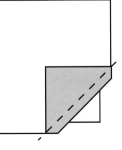

6. Press front-side and back-side triangles toward corner, so right side of fabric is seen.

Rectangles 1 through 6:

1. Pair up front sides and back sides.

2. Layer fabric and batting. With back fabric right-side down, place batting in center and place front fabric right side up.

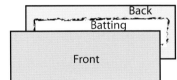

3. Press layers together with steam.

4. Place Adhesive Quilting Guide 1⅜" to the right of sewing machine needle.

5. Quilt down each side of the rectangles (total of two rows per rectangle).

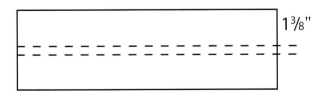

1⅜"

Sashings 7 and 8:

1. Quilt in the same manner as Rectangles 1 through 6.

Note: Because sashings are long, pin layers together to keep them in place while quilting.

135

First Border:

Stitch suggestion: A zigzag 0.5 mm wide and 3.0 mm long will give the appearance of hand quilting, looking a little wobbly.

Thread suggestion: Thread matching fabric on top and 39 g dark purple variegated yarn in bobbin.

Note: Because the border pieces are long, pin layers together to keep them in place.

1. Layer fabric and batting. With back fabric right-side down, place batting in center and place front fabric right side up.

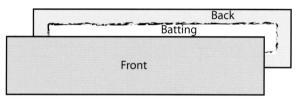

2. Press layers together with steam.

3. Place Adhesive Quilting Guide 4" to the right of sewing machine needle.

4. Quilt down the middle of borders.

5. Channel-stitch a row one presser-foot width away on both sides of the middle quilting.

6. Channel-stitch another row one presser-foot width away on both sides of the previous quilting (total of five rows).

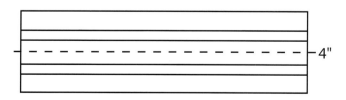

7. Place Adhesive Quilting Guide 1⅜" to the right of the sewing machine needle, as shown in diagram in next column.

8. Quilt down each side of the border.

Thread change: 39 g beige variegated yarn in bobbin. (Switch to a contrast thread color in bobbin to enhance decorative stitching.)

9. Using a decorative stitch of your choice, quilt one row toward the middle on both sides of the border, as shown in the diagram.

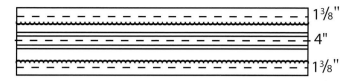

Second Border:

Thread suggestion: Match thread to fabric for front side and back side.

Note: Second border consists of three sections pieced together lengthwise.

1. Layer fabric and batting. With back fabric right-side down, place batting in center and place front fabric right side up.

2. Press layers together with steam. Pin layers together, if necessary.

3. Quilt in the same manner as Rectangles 1 through 6.

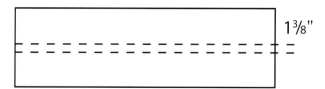

Third Border:

1. Quilt in the same manner as Rectangles 1 through 6.

Fourth Border:

Thread suggestion: Match thread to fabric for front side and back side.

1. Layer fabric and batting. With back fabric right-side down, place batting in center and place front fabric right side up.

2. Press layers together with steam.

3. Place Adhesive Quilting Guide 4½" to the right of the sewing machine needle.

4. Quilt down the middle of the border.

5. Channel-stitch a row one presser-foot width away from the previous quilting.

6. Repeat rows of channel stitching to within 1⅜" from edge of fabric, alternating directions to compensate for fabric shifting.

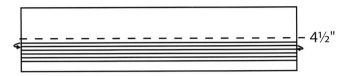

Note: Because the widths of presser feet vary, the number of quilting rows will vary.

7. Channel-stitch the other half of the border in the same manner.

Assembly Instructions

Insert topstitch needle into your sewing machine. Seam allowances will be finished on the front side using Highway and One-Way Street procedures.

Note: Use a 1" seam allowance when sewing the quilted pieces together.

Thread suggestion: Dark red variegated 40-weight cotton on top and dark purple variegated 40-weight cotton in bobbin.

Center Squares:

1. See quilt diagram on Page 142 to arrange center squares and center rectangles in the proper order.

2. With back sides together, sew Rectangle 1 to the top and bottom of center squares.

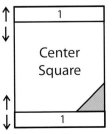

Note: Triangle placement will vary.

3. Press seams open on front side; then press the back side.

4. Finish seams using the Highway procedure. (See Techniques, Page 21.)

5. With back sides together, sew Rectangle 3 to the sides of center squares.

6. Press the back side; then press all seam allowances on front side toward the outside edges.

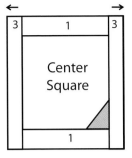

7. Finish seams using the One-Way Street procedure. (See Techniques, Page 22.)

8. With back sides together, sew Rectangle 5 to the top and bottom of center squares.

9. Press the back side; then press all seam allowances on front side toward the outside edges.

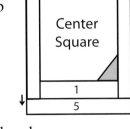

10. Finish seams using the One-Way Street procedure.

Note: You will have 12 extra Rectangle 5 pieces.

Center Rectangles:

1. With back sides together, sew Rectangle 2 to the top and bottom of center rectangles.

Note: Triangle placement will vary.

2. Press seams open on front side; then press the back side.

3. Finish seams using the Highway procedure.

4. With back sides together, sew Rectangle 4 to the sides of center rectangles.

5. Press the back side; then press all seam allowances on front side toward the outside edges.

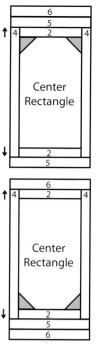

6. Finish seams using the One-Way Street procedure.

Row 2, Row 5, Row 8 and Row 11:

1. With back sides together, sew remaining Rectangle 5 or Rectangle 6, as indicated in the diagram, to the top and bottom of center rectangles in Row 2, Row 5, Row 8, and Row 11 only.

2. Press the back side; then press all seam allowances on front side toward the outside edges.

3. Finish seams using the One-Way Street procedure.

Attaching Center Rectangles in Row 2, Row 5, Row 8, and Row 11:

1. With back sides together, sew center rectangles together in Row 2, Row 5, Row 8 and Row 11. Be sure to align intersections. (See Techniques, Page 23.)

2. Press seams open on front side; then press the back side.

3. Finish seams using the Highway procedure.

Row 2
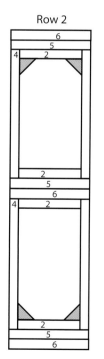

Row 5
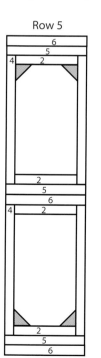

Row 8
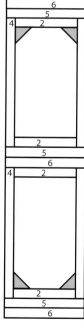

Row 11
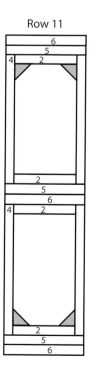

Attaching Center Squares and Center Rectangles in Row 1, Row 3, Row 4, Row 6, Row 7, Row 9, Row 10, and Row 12:

1. With back sides together, sew center square to center rectangle to center square. Be sure to align intersections.

2. Press the back side; then press all seam allowances on front side toward Rectangle 5.

3. Finish seams using the One-Way Street procedure.

Attaching Sashing 7:

1. With back sides together, sew Sashing 7 to connect Rows 1 through 12, as shown on Page 140. Be sure to align intersections. Fold and finish each seam before adding another row.

2. Press the back side; then press all seam allowances on front side toward sashing.

3. Finish seams using the One-Way Street procedure.

4. With back sides together, sew Sashing 7 to the outside edges of Row 1, Row 6, Row 7, and Row 12, as shown on Page 140.

5. Press the back side; then press all seam allowances on front side toward the outside edges.

6. Finish seams using the One-Way Street procedure.

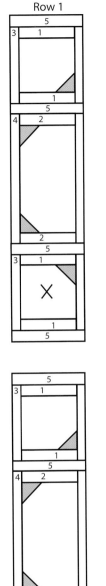

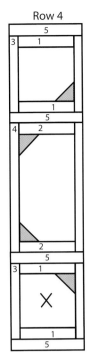

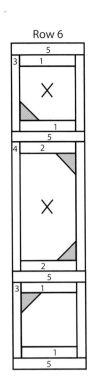

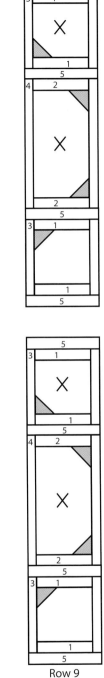

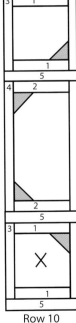

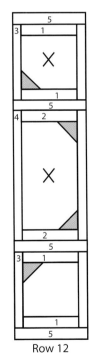

Row 1   Row 3   Row 4   Row 6

Row 7   Row 9   Row 10   Row 12

Applying Sashing 8:

1. With back sides together, sew Sashing 8 to connect the top quilt section and the bottom quilt section.

2. Press the back side; then press seam allowances on front side toward the sashing.

3. Finish seam using the One-Way Street procedure.

4. With back sides together, sew Sashing 8 to top and bottom of quilt.

5. Press the back side; then press seam allowances on front side toward the outside edges.

6. Finish seam using the One-Way Street procedure.

Applying First Border:

1. With back sides together, sew first border to sides of quilt.

2. Press the back side; then press seam allowances on front side toward border.

3. Finish seam using the One-Way Street procedure.

4. Sew first border to top and bottom of quilt in same manner.

5. Attach flange insert to create a Boardwalk in the quilt. (For instructions, see Techniques, Page 25.)

Applying Second Border:

Note: It takes three strips of fabric to complete each border piece, as shown in diagram on Page 142.

1. With back sides together, sew two strips together.

2. Press seams open on front side; then press the back side.

Thread change: 39 g dark purple variegated yarn in bobbin.

3. Finish seams using the Highway procedure.

4. With back sides together, sew the third strip to the previous strips.

5. Press seams open on front side; then press the back side.

6. Finish seams using the Highway procedure.

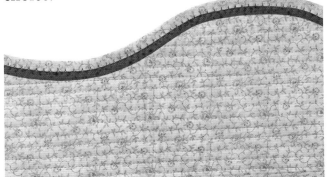

Thread change: Dark purple variegated 40-weight cotton thread in bobbin.

7. With back sides together, sew second border to sides of quilt.

8. Press the back side; then press seam allowances on front side toward border.

Note: The flange insert should be double-folded back to the original seam at the same time that you fold the seam allowances of the border. This is the Boardwalk.

9. Finish seam using the Highway procedure.

10. Sew second border to top and bottom of quilt in the same manner.

Applying Third Border:

1. With back sides together, sew third border to sides of quilt.

2. Press the back side; then press seam allowances on front side toward border.

3. Finish seam using the One-Way Street procedure.

4. Sew third border to top and bottom of quilt in the same manner.

Applying Fourth Border:

Thread change: Match thread in top part of sewing machine to fabric.

Note: The fourth border needs to be applied before sculpturing the raw edges. Sculptured edges are optional. You may finish the quilt using the binding of your choice.

Sculptured edge with Sidewalk Binding

1. With back sides together, sew fourth border to sides of quilt.

2. Press the back side; then press seam allowances on front side toward border.

3. Finish seam using the One-Way Street procedure.

4. Sew fourth border to top and bottom of quilt in the same manner.

5. To sculpture edges of the quilt, see instructions in Techniques, Page 26.

6. To add Sidewalk Binding to the quilt, see instructions in Binding section at end of this book.

Row 1   Row 2   Row 3   Row 4   Row 5   Row 6

Row 7   Row 8   Row 9   Row 10   Row 11   Row 12

1st Border

Boardwalk

2nd Border (3 strips sewn together)

3rd Border   4th Border

Keep scallop 1" from raw edge

X = Mirror imaged centers

Finished Two Dear Darling Daughters Bed Quilt Diagram
(87" x 103")

142

Part Four
Finishing Up

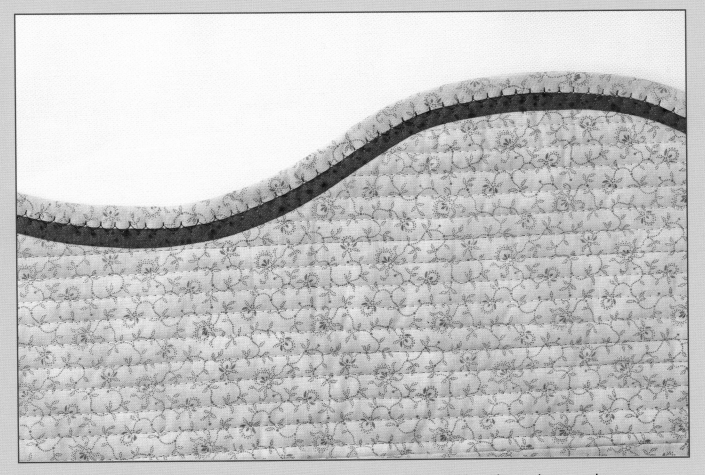

Every Cotton Theory project requires some kind of binding. This photo shows a close-up of Sidewalk Binding. Learn more about bindings on the following pages.

Binding

French-Fold Binding

Machine-applied French-fold binding is the easiest type of binding to use to finish your quilt, and it adds durability to the quilt's edges.

Note: Binding strips usually are 2½" wide.

Before adding binding, trim ⅝" from the raw edges of your project, leaving a ⅜" seam allowance on all sides. Trimming is necessary because Cotton Theory projects have no batting within 1" of raw edges.

1. With right sides together, piece together binding strips with mitered seams (45-degree angle), as shown in diagram.

2. Stitch a diagonal line across the two strips.

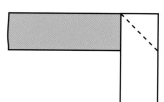

3. Trim the excess to ¼".

4. Press the seam open so binding lies flat.

The Magic Triangle:

The Magic Triangle will help you make a mitered seam when stitching the beginning and ending binding tails together.

1. With wrong side facing up, fold up one end of binding to form a triangle and press with steam iron.

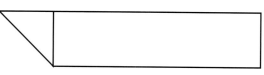

2. With wrong sides together, fold binding in half lengthwise and press.

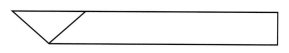

Applying Binding to Quilt:

Note: Binding will be sewn to the back side of project, then folded to the front side and machine-stitched in place.

1. With raw edges even, sew binding to back of quilt with a ⅜" seam, beginning in the middle of one side and leaving the first 6" of binding free of stitching.

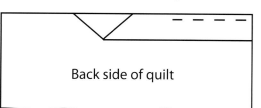

Back side of quilt

2. Stop stitching ⅜" from the corner and backstitch.

3. Remove quilt from sewing machine.

4. Fold binding up, creating a 45-degree angle, and press with fingers.

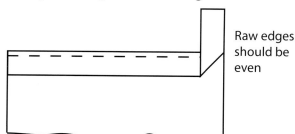

Raw edges should be even

5. Fold binding straight down, with the folded edge of the binding even with the quilt edge (45-degree angle will be hidden.)

6. Using a ⅜" seam, begin stitching at the fold and backstitch.

Folded edge

7. Continue applying binding in this manner around all corners.

8. Stop sewing about 6" from starting point, leaving the last 6" of binding free of stitching.

9. Tuck the ending binding tail inside the beginning binding tail, where the Magic Triangle is pressed in place. Open up binding.

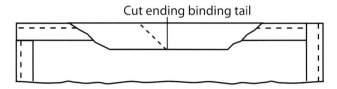

Cut ending binding tail

10. Cut ending binding tail even with right-hand side of Magic Triangle.

11. Pin ending binding tail to Magic Triangle, matching top and side edges.

12. Sew together at 45-degree angle on creased, diagonal line of Magic Triangle.

13. Trim the excess to ¼", and press seam open.

14. Refold binding in half.

15. Stitch the remaining seam.

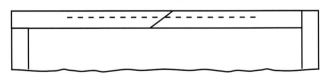

16. Press binding flat toward the outside.

Machine-Stitching Binding in Place

Note: Fold top binding first; then fold the left side binding.

1. Fold top binding to front side, back to the original seam. Finger-press folded binding at corner, forming a 45-degree angle.

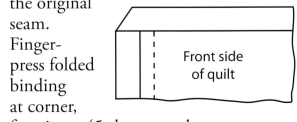

Front side of quilt

Note: It may be necessary to hand tack the binding in the corners. You will be using a decorative stitch or zigzag to secure binding in place.

2. Fold side binding to front side, back to the original seam.

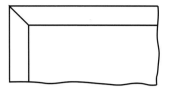

3. With a decorative stitch of your choice, stitch in the ditch (on the original seam) to sew binding in place.

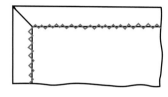

Bias Binding

Trim raw edges of quilt before applying binding. Refer to each project's instructions for details on trimming.

Certain fabrics, such as checks and plaids, become more attractive when cut on the true bias. Also, bias binding, which is cut on a 45-degree angle, is required when binding scalloped edges.

Cutting Instructions:

Remove selvages. A ⅝-yard strip of fabric will yield two 21" squares.

1. Cut a 21" x 21" square (unless instructed otherwise).

2. Fold in half diagonally (do not press the fold).

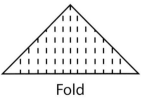

Fold

3. Place fold on a horizontal grid line on cutting mat.

4. Place tip of triangle on a vertical grid line on cutting mat.

5. Cut binding strips at the width required for your project.

Note: These binding strips have mitered ends ready to sew together.

6. With right sides together, sew bias strips end to end with a ¼" seam.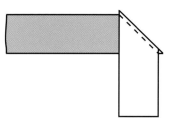

7. Press seams open.

8. Refer to French-Fold Binding on Page 144 for instructions on applying binding to quilt.

Reversible Binding

When constructing reversible quilts, you may not have a compatible binding fabric for both sides of the project. Reversible binding consists of two fabrics sewn together so the fabrics coordinate with each side.

Note: Binding strips are cut 2¼" wide for the front side and 1¼" wide for the back.

Before adding binding, trim ½" from the raw edges of your project, leaving a ½" seam allowance on all sides. Trimming is necessary because Cotton Theory projects have no batting within 1" of the raw edges.

1. With right sides together, piece together front-side binding strips with mitered seams (45-degree angle), as shown at top of next column.

The top of this tote bag is a good example of reversible binding — pink on one side and orange on the other.

2. Stitch a diagonal line across the two strips.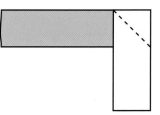

3. Trim the excess to ¼".

4. Press the seam open.

5. With right sides together, piece together back-side binding strips with mitered seams. Repeat Steps 2 through 4.

Joining Front-Side and Back-Side Binding:

1. With right sides together, sew front-side binding to back-side binding lengthwise with a ¼" seam and a short stitch length (2.0 mm).

2. Set the seam by pressing the stitching.

3. Press seam open.

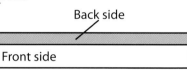

Back side

Front side

The Magic Triangle:

The Magic Triangle will help you make a mitered seam when stitching the beginning and ending binding tails together.

1. With wrong side facing up, fold down one end of binding to form a triangle and press.

Wrong side

2. With wrong sides together, fold binding in half lengthwise and press.

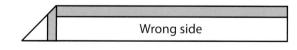

Front side

Applying Binding to Quilt:

Note: Binding will be sewn to the back side of project and then folded to the front side.

1. With raw edges even and seam facing down, sew both layers of binding to back side of quilt with ½" seam, beginning in center on one side and leaving first 6" of binding free of stitching.

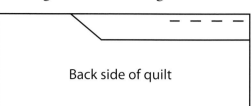

Back side of quilt

2. Stop stitching ½" from the corner, and then backstitch.

3. Remove quilt from sewing machine.

4. Fold binding up, making a 45-degree angle, and press with fingers.

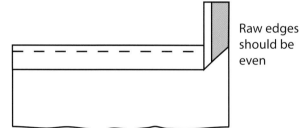

Raw edges should be even

5. Fold binding straight down, with the folded edge of the binding even with the quilt edge (45-degree angle will be hidden.)

6. Using a ½" seam, begin stitching at the fold and backstitch.

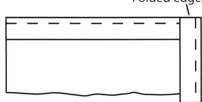

Folded edge

7. Continue applying binding in this manner around all corners.

8. Stop sewing 6" from the start, leaving last 6" of binding free of stitching.

9. Tuck the ending binding tail inside the beginning binding tail, where Magic Triangle is located. Open up binding.

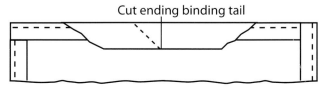

Cut ending binding tail

10. Cut ending binding tail even with right-hand side of Magic Triangle.

11. Pin ending binding tail to Magic Triangle, matching top and side edges.

12. Sew together at 45-degree angle on creased, diagonal line of Magic Triangle.

13. Trim excess to ¼" and press seam open.

14. Refold binding in half.

15. Stitch the remaining seam.

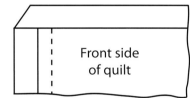

16. Press binding flat toward the outside.

Machine-Stitching Binding in Place:

Note: You will see the reversible binding starting to take effect. Fold top binding first; then fold left side binding.

1. Fold top binding to front side, back to original seam. Finger-press folded binding at corner, forming a 45-degree angle.

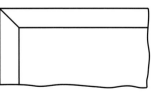

Front side of quilt

Note: It may be necessary to hand tack binding in corners. You will be using a zigzag or decorative stitch to secure binding in place.

2. Fold side binding to front side, back to original seam. (Remaining binding should be folded in same manner as Steps 1 and 2.)

3. With a decorative stitch of your choice, stitch in the ditch (on the original seam) to sew binding in place.

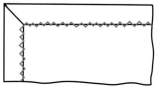

Highway Binding

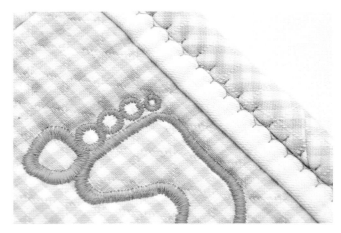

This close-up illustrates Highway binding.

Highway binding is a double-folded flange sewn to the raw edges of a quilt before machine-applying the binding. It gives the appearance of the Highway Cotton Theory seam when stitched in place.

In this book, Highway Binding is used on Two Little Tots Bath Mat. Strips are 3" wide.

Before adding binding, trim ½" from the raw edges of your project, leaving a ½" seam allowance on all sides. Trimming is necessary because Cotton Theory projects have no batting within 1" of the raw edges.

Steps 1 through 4 are required for large projects. Otherwise, skip to Step. 5.

1. With right sides together, piece together flange strips with mitered seams (45-degree angle).

2. Stitch a diagonal line across the two strips.

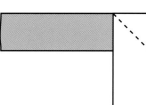

3. Trim excess to ¼".

4. Press the seam open.

5. Fold flange in half lengthwise and press.

Note: Flange will be applied to the front side. It will not appear on back side.

6. Starting with left-hand side of quilt, place raw edges of flange even with raw edges of quilt.

7. Machine baste a scant ½" from raw edges.

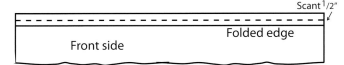

8. Double-fold the ends only back to the original seam (fold ¼" and fold again), as shown in diagram.

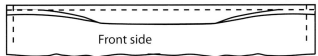

9. Machine baste these ends in place a scant ½".

Note: Do not double-fold the entire flange. It will be folded later when applying binding

10. Apply flange to right-hand side and to top and bottom of quilt in the same manner.

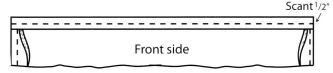

11. Double-fold the ends only back to the original seam, as shown in diagram.

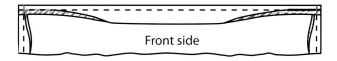

12. Machine baste the ends in place a scant ½".

13. Refer to French fold binding on Page 144 for instructions on applying binding to quilt.

Note: Due to extra fabric layers in Two Little Tots Bath Mat, the binding is cut 3" wide. You will sew binding with ½"seam.

Note: Before stitching binding in place with decorative stitch, double-fold flange to the original seam. Flange should meet the binding, looking like a Highway seam.

Sidewalk Binding

Just as a sidewalk is a path along the side of a road, Sidewalk Binding creates a path along the side of the actual binding. The Sidewalk Binding is an additional fabric added before the final binding. (See photo on Page 143.)

In this book, Sidewalk Binding is used on Two Dear Darling Daughters on Page 127.

Note: When applying Sidewalk or other binding to a quilt with sculptured edges, the binding needs to be cut on the bias. (See Page 145.)

Applying the Sidewalk:

1. With right sides together, piece together 1¼" bias insert strips end to end (at least 400") with a ¼" mitered seam (45-degree angle).

2. Press seams open.

3. Fold strip in half lengthwise and press with steam iron to set a crease line.

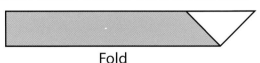

Fold

4. Open strip back up.

5. Fold and press a ¼" hem on the short side.

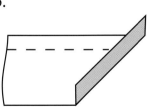

Note: Make sure batting goes to the raw edges of your quilt. Trim raw edges, if necessary.

6. With right sides together and opened flat, place bias insert on the front side of quilt with raw edges even.

7. Starting in the middle of one side and leaving about 6" free of stitching at the beginning, sew insert to front side of quilt with a ⅝" seam. (You will be sewing down the middle, along your creased line.)

Front side of quilt

8. Stop sewing about 12" from starting point.

9. Overlap the the beginning and ending strip.

10. Sew on the creased line.

Sew together and trim

Front side of quilt

11. Trim excess strip to ¼".

12. Stitch the remaining strip in place.

13. Press strip toward the outside (in half). Raw edges will be even.

Note: This is the Sidewalk.

14. Refer to French-Fold Binding on Page 144 for instructions on applying single-fold bias binding to quilt. (For single-fold bias binding, omit Step 2 under instructions titled The Magic Triangle. Do not fold binding in half.)

Front side of quilt

Note: Single-fold bias strips will perform best with scallops or sculptured edges.

About the author

Betty Cotton is a quilting entrepreneur who invented Cotton Theory quilting in 2001 and received a patent on it in 2004. She lives in Eau Claire, Wisconsin, and owns a quilt shop in nearby Osseo, Wis.

Ordering Information

Supplies

Cotton Theory products
Adhesive Quilting Guide
Cotton Theory Batting
Columbine Embroidery Design
Cotton Theory Patterns
Cotton Theory Instructional DVD
39 g variegated yarn
2 mm silk ribbon

OESD, Inc. Embroidery
Left Hand Print NV255
Right Hand Print NV256
Left Foot Print NV258
Right Foot Print NV257

Pfaff Embroidery
Pfaff 347/Design 10
Pfaff 354 Fine Line Art, Design 3
Pfaff 354 Fine Line Art, Design 6

Cactus Punch Embroidery
Pine Bough Sprig,
    Cactus Punch (Sig 45)
Hand Sewing,
    Cactus Punch Quilting Vol. 4
Porridge,
    Cactus Punch Quilting Vol. 4
Mine!,
    Cactus Punch Quilting Vol. 4

Synthetic suede
Iron Quick Teflon

Where to Order

Cotton Theory® LLC
13900 7th Street, PO Box 22
Osseo, WI 54758
Phone: (715) 597-2883 or (800) 673-8075
E-mail: sales@quiltyard.com
Internet: www.quiltyard.com

Oklahoma Embroidery Supply & Design, Inc.
www.EmbroideryOnline.com.

Local Pfaff dealers

Local sewing machine dealers

Nancy's Notions, Beaver Dam, Wis.
www.nancysnotions.com